The Present Truth

Thoughts of a Musing Christian

Martin Murphy

The Present Truth

Copyright © 2012 by Martin Murphy

Cover Design by Mike Waters for Framework Productions, Inc.

Published by: Theocentric Publishing Group
1069 Main Street
Chipley, Florida 32428

http://www.theocentricpublishing.com

All rights reserved. No part of this book may be reproduced or transmitted in any form or by any means without written permission of the author.

Unless otherwise noted Scripture is taken from the New King James Version. Copyright © 1979, 1980, 1982 by Thomas Nelson, Inc. Used by permission. All rights reserved.

Library of Congress Control Number: 2012934530

ISBN 9780983244172

To

The twentieth century church

Sine qua non

Preface

The history of the human race has a long history of despair and defeat. I've lived long enough to see people suffer mental and emotional pain as a result of despair and defeat. They ultimately lose the battle to death. The only salvation for me was that God intervened, gave me the ability to believe, and the assurance that there is more to life than despair and defeat. The present truth is that God was, God is, and God always will tell the truth and be the truth.

The grand scheme and history of the Christian religion defined in the Old Testament Israel and the New Testament Church has struggled along with the entire human race to find the present truth that always was, is and will be. I'm writing "The Present Truth" because it is what I presently see, that always was and probably always will be, until the curtain closes for this present life.

Twenty plus years ago I read a book entitled "Amusing Ourselves to Death" by Neil Postman. The word "amusing" captured my attention. I had always understood it in reference to entertainment, especially something comical. The desire to find pleasure in amusement creates a monster that will never satisfy an inquiring mind. However, the word "muse" actually refers to serious thinking, contemplation, and meditation. I decided then that amusement in the western culture had captivated the attention of the mind and I was no exception. I realized that "musing" is the goal for a rational mind. There is wisdom in musing, but amusement leads to an empty mind. The essays contained in this book are "Thoughts of a Musing Christian."

These are essays written over the past twenty years because of some encounter with biblical doctrine, theological inquiry, or philosophical contemplation. I wrote some of them because I like to write. The research behind them was for my own spiritual growth. They capsulize some of the thoughts of this musing Christian.

Religious thought fascinated me from my youth. During the formative years of my adolescence, a young minister moved into the community. He took an interest in the young people, so I attended church for a while. He was killed in an automobile accident. I could not understand why a good God would allow this tragedy. For the next twenty years, I assumed an agnostic position. I didn't believe or disbelieve, I just didn't know. Over that twenty-year period scores of professing Christians, many of them preachers, tried to amuse me with their religious opinions. When I was thirty-two years old, I had an encounter with Jesus Christ while reading the Bible. The Lord opened my heart to believe the gospel and believe that the Bible was the ultimate and final authority for life and faith. It was by the power of the Holy Spirit that I was able to believe what was formally unbelievable.

I have devoted the past thirty-three years musing the meaning of life. While musing, I enjoy a favorable relationship with God because of Jesus Christ by the power of the Holy Spirit.

Martin Murphy
March 15, 2012

Table of Contents

1. State of the Christian 1
2. State of the Church 9
3. Nature of the Church 17
4. Purpose of the Church 23
5. Mission and Ministry 33
6. Invite Unbelievers to Church 41
7. Invite Believers to Worship 49
8. Why? 61
9. Natural Man 69
10. Sin Is... 79
11. Man-Made Religion 87
12. Doctrinal Integrity 97
13. Anger 105
14. Marriage 111
15. Education 117
16. Looking Back 127
17. Death 135
18. Brief Comments 139

1. State of the Christian

But I trust in the Lord Jesus to send Timothy to you shortly, that I also may be encouraged when I know your state for I have no one like-minded, who will sincerely care for your state. For all seek their own, not the things which are of Christ Jesus. But you know his proven character, that as a son with his father he served with me in the gospel.
Philippians 2:19-22

Christians must examine themselves in light of the Word of God. "I wish Mr. (or Mrs.) X could have heard that sermon. It's just what he (or she) needed," said Mr. Y as he shook the pastor's hand after the worship service. Christian, examine yourself, not your neighbor, the church, or the world. Examine your real self, your inward self, not the outward appearance. Examine yourself at the present time, not the past, nor what you expect to be in the future. Examine yourself according to the Word of God, the whole counsel of God, not according to a spoof text to defend your views and not according to your own feeble feelings. On the other hand beware of the elite super-spiritual Christian because he or she is always ready to condemn your spiritual journey. In fact, some of them are ready to stone you to death if they judge you to be a sinner.

The popular concept today is culture comparison. How well are we keeping up with the culture around us? To bad that so many have on glasses so dark they can't see reality. As in the days of the apostle Paul, Christians live "in the midst of a crooked and perverse generation" (Philippians 2:15). Christians should be ever aware that the culture looks at the Christian with critical eyes. When they look at Christians they see the church. Do our unbelieving friends see grumbling, complaining, and divisive church members? Visit most any TV sitcom and you may see some startling resemblance to the modern evangelical church.

The apostle Paul gave the Philippian Christians explicit instructions for living in the culture that despised Christianity. Paul described the condition of the culture during the first century as "a crooked and perverse generation." The word "crooked" referred to people who were bent out of shape. It literally means they were disfigured. Perverted signifies that they had turned aside from that which was considered to be right or good. The culture was full of violence and uncontrollable passions seeking happiness. It was a culture that embraced irrationalism and anti-intellectualism. Sounds like the world we live in today. Even though God saves His people from the crooked and depraved culture, God's people still live in the crooked and depraved culture. There is a perennial question that all Christians have to ask. How are Christians supposed to live in this non-Christian world?

"Shine as lights in the world, holding forth the word of life" so says the apostle Paul. Holding forth the word of life is certain to provoke the crooked and perverse generation. It must be remembered that the "word of life" is not a pie-in-the-sky promise. The word of life is the absolute truth. It comes from God. You must have the truth if you expect to be actively engaged in the culture.

The question that plagues every religious sector, every philosophical proposition, and every cultural milieu is "what is truth?" From the 18th century enlightenment until the 20th century the Heisenberg uncertainty principle, the concept of relativity, attempted to explain truth to the public square. The blame does not properly belong to any one philosophical discipline, or the concepts of modernity or post modernity. The blame lies in the doctrine of sin. The effect of sin on the intellect is the reason for all the conflict over truth. Not only the intellect, but the will represents the changeable nature that accompanies the confused sinful mind. There are times when

1. State of the Christian

truth is neither easy nor convenient to accept. To acquire and understand truth requires hard work. But not even hard work will solve all truth propositions. The discovery of truth depends on the source that reveals truth. To put it another way, the knowledge of truth is not possible without divine illumination. When the Jews, the professing people of God, confronted Jesus they said "We were not born of fornication; we have one Father – God" (John 8:41). Jesus responded with a statement about the truth.

> If God were your Father, you would love Me, for I proceeded forth and came from God; nor have I come of Myself, but He sent Me. Why do you not understand My speech? Because you are not able to listen to My word. You are of your father the devil, and the desires of your father you want to do. He was a murderer from the beginning, and does not stand in the truth, because there is no truth in him. When he speaks a lie, he speaks from his own resources, for he is a liar and the father of it. But because I tell the truth, you do not believe Me. Which of you convicts Me of sin? And if I tell the truth, why do you not believe Me? He who is of God hears God's words; therefore you do not hear, because you are not of God. (John 8:42-47)

Unbelievers may know some truth, but only by the generous providence of God. The cultural elites have successfully deceived several generations into believing that truth is so abstract that it becomes practically useless. Mental assent is sufficient for most and for the rest if truth really surfaces, it is to be put on a shelf so it will not divide the ranks.

So where does this leave the state of the Christian? It leaves the Christian standing on the edge of a cliff about to fall into a neo dark age. It is for that reason that God's people need to wake up before it is too late. Turn your back on the darkness and "shine as light" so says the apostle Paul.

Don't pretend to be Christian. If you're not a Christian admit it and seek the Lord while He may be found.

Debate and defend the truth as God illumines your mind. The great statesman, Henry Clay, was about to introduce a certain bill in Congress when a friend said, "If you do, Clay, it will kill your chance for the presidency." "But is the measure right" Clay said, and being assured it was right he said, "I would rather be right than president."

Where are the men like Henry Clay? Where is the culture that once believed that truth counts? I've encountered deep resistance to truth. I've known and encountered professing Christians who are experts at making a proposition sound like truth and take pride in it. For instance, someone could say there is a squirrel in the living room. Taken out of context that might mean that a squirrel is in my living room, when in reality (truth) there is no squirrel in my living room. I had one man tell me once "I take the ninth commandment too seriously." As a sinner, just like you, I might break the ninth commandment, but how could a Christian say that someone took the ninth commandment too seriously? A statement like that is easy to understand, if you understand that the state of the Christian is more inclined to pietism than to the whole counsel of God. This is not the time for pietism or timidity.

The solution is simple and complex at the same time, but not in the same relationship. The Word of God tells us that it is God who began a good work in us and it is God who "will perfect it until the day of Jesus Christ." If a professing Christian is not really a Christian then the culture is more comforting than the truth. If a professing Christian is a Christian the truth will be more important than the culture.

The way to make sure you "hold forth the word of truth" is to consult the ultimate authority for faith and life. The Word of God must be your delight, your confidence, your love,

1. State of the Christian

and the light to your path. Christians must conclude as the Psalmist did to "esteem right all Thy precepts concerning everything, I hate every false way" (Psalm 119:128).

Since the state of the Christian reflects the state of the church, it is necessary to admit to the truth of the state of the church. The church has fallen on hard times. Its ministers are no longer respected as honorable men called to speak for the dignity and glory of God. There was a time in this country when the pastor had a profound influence on the life of the church as well as the community.

The orthodox doctrines of the Christian religion once held in high esteem, are more often than not, and considered a hindrance to the growth of the church. Michael Horton makes the point that "when evangelicals gave up Calvinistic orthodoxy, they abandoned an intellectual system which provided families, churches, communities, cities, schools and trades with a way of looking at the world - a biblical way of doing so" (*Made in America*, by Michael Horton).

Godly pastors are needed for reformation. Pastors seeking biblical reformation in the modern church are very likely to be turned aside by "well intentioned dragons." There are people in the church who have what are often referred to as good intentions, although they are unbiblical intentions. They want to preserve some tradition or promote some good program that may merit attention in another situation. The list of their "good intentions" are too numerous to mention, but good intentions must stand the test of Holy Scripture. If you seek biblical reformation, do not be surprised when the enemy, maybe within, maybe without, attacks you with every poisonous dart he can find. Your source of strength must come from the Holy Spirit of God, because godly pastors seeking biblical reformation are not very popular.

The apostle Paul experienced a similar problem. In Paul's letter to the Philippians he encouraged the Philippian Church to continue the reformation. Paul was not present with the Philippian Christians and he wanted to send Timothy to the church. The historical narrative that follows is a sad commentary on the church during Paul's ministry. Paul said, "For I have no one else of kindred spirit who will genuinely be concerned for your welfare. For they all seek after their own interests, not those of Christ Jesus" (Philippians 2:20-21). Paul may have used hyperbole (an intentional exaggeration) to emphasize the need for the church to be likeminded. It is a sad day when so few have an interest in Christ Jesus.

What made Timothy stand out as the only one who was like minded with Paul? Obviously Paul knew that Timothy was an eager student of Holy Scripture. Paul had already instructed Timothy to "continue in the things you have learned" (2 Timothy 3:14) and to "retain the standard of sound words which you have heard from me" (2 Timothy 1:13). The truth from God's Word was the standard for Paul and it was the standard for Timothy. It must be the standard for anyone seeking biblical reformation.

It is godly pastors like Timothy who have a spiritual interest in others rather than self interest. "For they all seek the things of themselves, not the things of Christ Jesus" (Philippians 2:21). Christians like Timothy will be the instruments of reformation for the church. Who are these self seekers mentioned by the apostle Paul? I think they are mentioned earlier in Paul's letter. Paul did not speak very well of these self-seekers in the church at Philippi. Paul said, "Most of the brethren, trusting in the Lord because of my imprisonment, have far more courage to speak the Word of God without fear. Some to be sure, are preaching Christ even from envy and strife, but some also from good will; the latter do it out of love, knowing that I am appointed for the defense of the gospel; the former proclaim Christ out of selfish ambition, rather than from pure motives, thinking to cause me distress in my imprisonment" (Philippians1:14-17).

1. State of the Christian

The evil of self-seeking is a destructive force in the church, as it always has been. Many professing Christians seem more interested in themselves than they are the kingdom of God. They want people to notice them. They want to see how much authority they can exert over others. Jesus speaking to the Pharisees said, "but they do all their deeds to be noticed by men, they love the place of honor at banquets and being called by men Rabbi" (Matthew 23:5). The Pharisees were the religious leaders in Israel, the covenant people of God. The church has professing Christians who smile outwardly, but inwardly there is a little voice that says, "Notice me and see how important I am."

Paul had confidence that Timothy was not a self-seeker, but on the contrary was like minded with Paul and would make a good candidate for continuing the good work of reformation in Philippi.

Another reason Paul wanted to send Timothy was that Timothy was pleased in seeking Christ. The opposite of self-seeking is Christ-seeking. In the absence of Paul's best disciple, what did the apostle do? Paul said, "I considered it necessary to send to you Epaphroditus." Maybe Epaphroditus was not gifted like Paul and Timothy, but Paul forgets the difference and speaks of Epaphroditus as Paul's equal. Paul does not contradict himself, nor does he compare Timothy to Epaphroditus. Paul could speak of Timothy the way he did because Timothy had been a very close companion of Paul through out his ministry, but Paul probably had little contact with Epaphroditus during the ten years since Paul had planted the church at Philippi.

Notice how Paul spoke of Epaphroditus and how it is evident that he had the marks of a pastor interested in the biblical reformation of the church. Paul calls Epaphroditus a necessary brother. He was interested in the care of other Christians. Epaphroditus was a necessary fellow worker and a necessary fellow soldier. He was engaged in spiritual warfare like the apostle Paul.

We find the example of three godly pastors and they have set the example for pastors in the church. Paul was a pastor with a passion for teaching other men, but never forgetting his personal responsibility. Timothy and Epaphroditus are examples of godly pastors who were biblical Reformers.

I ask you, did these men stand for something more than a comfortable pastorate? The answer is yes! They were willing to sacrifice.

The state of the Christian has not changed much through the centuries. There are new names, cultures have changed, technology has increased, but the report is much the same. We stand at the edge of the precipice. The culture is always ready to consume us or throw us off the cliff.

If we are afraid of what is before us, then we are sure to take the plunge individually, but God will always preserve His church. If we are willing to accept the responsibility to stand for the truth then we might suffer and according to the Word of God will suffer. Even so the state of the Christian will be semper reformanda (always reforming).

2. State of the Church

And He Himself gave some to be apostles, some prophets, some evangelists, and some pastors and teachers, for the equipping of the saints for the work of ministry, for the edifying of the body of Christ, till we all come to the unity of the faith and of the knowledge of the Son of God, to a perfect man, to the measure of the stature of the fullness of Christ; that we should no longer be children, tossed to and fro and carried about with every wind of doctrine, by the trickery of men, in the cunning craftiness of deceitful plotting, but, speaking the truth in love, may grow up in all things into Him who is the head—Christ...
Ephesians 4:11-15

The more I look at the church the less I see of the church. The more I look at the American culture, the more I see the church. It has not been too long since the Fundamentalists led the march to recover Christian ethics in a pagan society. Recover what? How can something be recovered that never existed? Untangling the facts from the fiction in the nineteenth and twentieth century church will be a noble task for the next generation of Christians. Today I'm not so much interested in how we got here. My interest is on the current state of the church.

With the risk of being called a pessimist, I will lay out what I believe to be the current state of the church at the beginning of the 21st century. The church is polarized. Theological ignorance abounds. Utilitarianism is the trend. Ecclesiastical intrigue is common as Sunday school. God's law is horribly misinterpreted. Moralism replaced justification by faith alone. There is a sense in which the church appears to be skating on a thin layer of ice, but God is sovereign. God has not taken a nap only to wake up and find the world and the church in such a mess that even God's people are lost. Every soul is exactly at the place that God appointed before the creation of the world. God's people should rejoice that they have been counted worthy of suffering for the sake of the Lord Jesus Christ. If my assessment of the church is true, what should we do as a suffering church?

Although we serve in a suffering church, we still seek peace, harmony, and unity for the church. Unfortunately, Christians often think that peace, harmony and unity are worth the sacrifice of biblical doctrine. The *Roman Catholic Evangelical Dialogue Statement* released in 1994 is a good example of how theologians want to heat up the doctrinal melting pot. The church is polarized, but "agreeing to disagree" will never solve the polarization. When two or more persons maintain different opinions, the only way to resolve the division is by some means of intelligent discourse. Intelligent argumentation is the only way to resolve doctrinal differences. Let me be quick to add and let me make it LOUD and CLEAR that I'm not advocating a perfect church. I'm not advocating that any statement of church doctrine is infallible. However, doctrinal statements, established by an in-depth study of the whole counsel of God, are necessary for peace and purity of the church. For example, the *Westminster Confession of Faith* is certainly a clear and precise statement of biblical doctrine. Yet the framers of that fine confession did not infer any infallibility for any confession, not even their own. "All Synods or councils since the apostles' times, whether general or particular, may err, and many have erred; therefore they are not to be made the rule of faith or practice, but to be used as a help in both" (*Westminster Confession of Faith*, 31.4). Westminster believed that the Bible was the only inspired "rule of faith and life." The suffering church must humbly submit to the authority of Scripture and use the tools of intelligent human discourse to resolve any division in the church.

2. State of the Church

While the postmodern American culture has tried to convince the church to deny absolute truth, the church must come to the knowledge of truth. The denial of absolute truth, if continued, will cripple the evangelical church in the western culture. Serious Bible study has been replaced by a dangerous, but popular remark; love an erring brother. Love is necessary for the Christian life, but what does it mean to love? A prominent man asked Jesus "what shall I do that I may inherit eternal life" (Mark 10:17)? During the course of their discussion, "Jesus looking at him, loved him" (Mark 10:21). Apparently love did not remedy the problem, because the Bible explains that the man "went away sorrowful" (Mark 10:22). Jesus loved him enough to tell the truth. It is time for individual Christians and the church collectively to lovingly and humbly, but courageously and vigorously speak the truth.

The Word of God instructs us to "speak the truth in love" (Ephesians 4:15). While the postmodern American culture cries "peace, peace," the church must cry out like the prophet Jeremiah "But there is no peace" (Jeremiah 6:14 and 8:11). Although the prophet Jeremiah spoke to Israel, the church underage, there is a sense in which the larger culture of the day was involved, because that culture was at war with Israel. God's covenant with His people will always have its effect with the culture. Sad to say, but the church has become like the culture. As the prophet said: "Everyone is given to covetousness; And from the prophet even to the priest, everyone deals falsely" (Jeremiah 6:13). Do the words of the prophet apply to the church and our culture of every generation? Yes, when denominational leaders agree to set aside sound doctrine found in the Word of God for the purpose of communion with the larger church community, the prophets and priests are dealing falsely. "It is on this margin that culture, seemingly entirely autonomous and detached, turns around and becomes a social and material force, a power of signification that discredits all claims to substantive grounds outside representation and this discrediting applies to political institutions, moral norms, social practices and economic structures" (*Postmodernist Culture*, by Steven Conner, p. 225). The philosophy of the culture is to dominate the church. The prophet Jeremiah described the church and culture precisely as we find it today.

Now we turn to the question, where on earth is the church or is it just in heaven? Why ask such a ridiculous question when we all know that the church of the living God is alive and well? The question comes to mind because it appears an ever-increasing number of evangelical churches are abandoning the true gospel for another gospel. I recall a conversation with a seminary student about how difficult it is to find a biblical church. During the conversation, he told me about a church he had attended the previous weekend. He explained how the preaching focused on Moralism and political activism.

Moralism refers to those who preach and teach that our Christian experience, the success or failure of it, depends on how well we obey the commandments of God. Obedience to the law of God is the goal in sanctification. Although it is a noble goal it will never be accomplished in this life time. Unfortunately, the church has grossly misinterpreted the Law of God and established rules according to an ungodly cultural agenda. Twentieth century Moralism is the modern version of first century Pharisaical law-keeping. It is the subjective law of man rather that objective law of God.

Political activism refers to the application of force in the political arena to get preference from politicians. Political activism, apart from individual Christians voting and exercising their constitutional rights, is just as wrong for the Christian church as it is for any organized lobby group. The purpose, mission, and ministry of the church does not call for political activism. The church ought to work to change the culture, not set up a Christian political dictatorship.

2. State of the Church

Christianity in the United States is not merely under attack from the cultural standards as much as it is under attack from those within its own ranks. The church does not need to fight over the cultural wars such as abortion, civil rights, or prayer in public schools. The church does not need to fret over law, education, or politics. Oh yes, all Christians must engage in the culture where God has placed them, but they must use God's plan to "subdue the earth." The Bible is the only source that reveals God's inspired plan. If Christians want to have an impact in Washington, then humbly submit to the law of God and present the gospel in its fullness by the power of the Holy Spirit. Engage in the cultural pursuit with a winsome countenance, but a passion for truth.

Several theologians have identified the radical shift in evangelical Christianity, especially since the culture wars have taken a prominent place in our society. After considerable inquiry, I am suggesting that the church is struggling with an identity crisis. The church consists of professing believers and their children. Many of them are struggling with an identity crisis. If the purpose, mission, and ministry of the church are not clearly defined, then confusion will follow; an identity crisis will emerge.

America is at war. The battlefields are raging with issues such as abortion, women's rights, gay rights, racial discrimination, education and list goes on and on. The sociologists and theologians refer to these issues as "cultural wars." These cultural wars demonstrate the Achilles heel of a democratic society. Every man, woman, and even the children want to control the circumstances of their lives and the world around them. If people feel violated, they cry, "I'm a victim." Victimizationalism is the public outcry reflecting the ungodly therapeutic influence in America. It is about a struggle for identity.

The basic assumption behind victimizationalism is the goodness and worth of self. It is built on the unbiblical notion that "I am and there is not one else besides me" (Isaiah 47:10). This unbiblical destructive worldview essentially says, "When something bad happens to me it is the fault of someone else. Since it is their fault, they must pay me some money."

Now Christians, let's hear the rest of the story. The Bible says, "Each one is tempted when he is drawn away by his own desires and enticed. Then, when desire has conceived, it gives birth to sin..." (James 1:14, 15). The sin nature always puts the blame on someone else just as Eve said, "the Devil made me do it" (Genesis 3:8-13). The unbiblical therapeutic enterprise attempts to avoid the sin problem and dwell on the goodness of man. They would do well to dwell on the goodness of God and the badness of man.

The trauma that accompanies a high-speed, high-tech, and high-performance society will affect how Christians relate to each other. The relationships break down when person A fails to communicate to person B's world of ideas and ideals. The identity crisis comes when one feels that no one understands his or her world. When individual Christians come to a crisis, the whole church will feel and express concern. "Do you not know that a little leaven leavens the whole lump of dough?" I will explain more about the purpose, mission and ministry of the church in later chapters.

The remedy for this complex dilemma rests in the fundamentals of the Christian faith, from which evangelicals have departed in recent church history. These fundamentals are essential for healthy churches. Let me be quick to clarify this point. "Healthy churches" is a phrase that means different things to different people. A healthy church refers to a congregation of God's people that defends the sound doctrine of the full counsel of God. However, it is defending, not with a mean spirit, but by truth in love.

The healthy church must have a source of authority. Something or someone must have the final word for any controversy. For the Christian, the Bible is that final source of

2. State of the Church

authority. The truth contained therein is not subject to contradiction. It is not relative truth. It does not mean one thing to one person and something else to another person. The Bible presents only absolute truth. To reject the Word of God is to reject the authority of God over your life and eternal destiny.

The rejection of God's authority takes us directly to the identity crisis. It has to do with our source of salvation. If Christians do not understand the source of their salvation, they will have misconceptions about their salvation. The identity crisis follows the misconception. I fear that so many otherwise godly Christians may be caught in the trap and forget the source of their salvation. If a person is not secure in the hands of God it will cause doubt and doubt leads to trauma. Personal therapeutic trauma leads to collective ecclesiastical trauma. The battlefields are raging in many of the mainline and evangelical denominations.

It appears that the battles within denominations have distracted the brethren from the spiritual battles to which they are called to fight. The Lord our God has called us to engage in spiritual warfare for the kingdom of God, not the kingdom of a denomination. A word to the wise; your salvation didn't come from a denomination or an ecclesiastical body. Salvation comes from the Lord God Almighty and it is Him we must serve. When Calvin was expelled from Geneva he said, "Had I been the servant of man, I should have received but poor wages. But happy for me it is that I am the servant of Him who never fails to give His servants that which He has promised them."

I am suggesting that an identity crisis prevails in the church. I am suggesting that too often Christians sit on the fence and wait to see which way the wind will blow. I am suggesting that the abuse of biblical authority has contributed to this identity crisis. I am suggesting that Christians get so enthralled with their private agenda that they overlook the source of their salvation. I am suggesting that we pray for God to enable us to believe, understand, and demonstrate that our identity is in Jesus Christ.

3. Nature of the Church

And He is the head of the body, the church, who is the beginning, the firstborn from the dead, that in all things He may have the preeminence.

Colossians 1:18

A diligent laborious study of the Bible is necessary to understand the doctrine of the church and to set aside the traditional false views of the church. First it is necessary to examine the general teaching then move to more specifics about the doctrine of the church.

The church consists of God's covenant people through every age and in every place on earth. The people of God in the Old Testament were called Israel; in the New Testament they are called the church. Plain and simple the people that belong to God in a favorable eternal relationship are the church. The grave mistake of many professing Christians is to refer to the church in terms of a physical piece of architecture. The building, mistakenly called the church, may be where God's people meet, but the building is not the church. There are various metaphors and figures in the Bible that describe the nature and character of the church.

An appropriate figure for the church is God's building (2 Corinthians 6:16). It is not a building made by man, but a building created in the image of God. Peter calls believers "living stones" which form and shape God's building. The apostle John used an agricultural metaphor to describe the nature of the church. The flock refers to the church in terms of the sheep and the shepherd (John 10:1-29). The family of God is another figure for the church. It has a Father and the children are called the household of believers. The Bride is a popular metaphor used to describe the church. The Bride honors and submits to the Groom and the Groom loves and sacrifices for, and teaches the Bride (Ephesians 5:22-29). There are other biblical metaphors such as the body, the field, the vineyard, and the kingdom that provide valuable information to help Christians understand the nature and character of the church. The nature of the church is inseparably connected to the nature of Jesus Christ. To ignore the true biblical teaching on the nature of the church is to ignore the Lord Jesus Christ.

The church is bi-dimensional. One dimension is the invisible church and the other is the visible church.

When we use the term "invisible church" it sounds like no one can see the invisible church. *Webster's Dictionary* defines invisible as "incapable of being seen" or "not presently apparent." The latter definition is applicable to the concept of the invisible church. The invisible church can be seen by the triune God, the angels and all the saints in heaven. The invisible church is often referred to as the church in heaven and there is an element of truth to that statement, but it must be refined for clarification. The Westminster Assembly during the 18th century described the invisible church as the "whole number of the elect that have been, are, or shall be... ." There are many members in the visible church. The true visible church on earth is also part of the invisible church (in heaven), but they are not actually in heaven proper. Although a distinction must be made between the invisible and visible church, true believers will be in both, but professing believers who are not saved will be in one; the visible church. The *Westminster Confession of Faith* describes the visible church as "catholic or universal under the Gospel (not confined to one nation, as before under the Law) consists of all those throughout the world that profess the true religion, together with their children" (Chap. 25, Sec. 1). I quote the Confession because I could not describe it any better.

Since Jesus Christ is the head of the Church only those who belong to Jesus Christ will find a home in the invisible

3. Nature of the Church

Church. It was the invisible Church for which Jesus Christ died. The union and communion of the true believer to Christ is a spiritual and invisible relation until the final judgment and the resurrection of the dead.

Augustine and Luther used the term "invisible church" because they believed it helps us relate to the invisible aspects of God's grace through the work of the Holy Spirit. The invisible church is the church that God sees in its perfected form. This dimension of the church should bring comfort to all Christians as they anticipate the eternal communion with the God of heaven and earth.

The Roman Catholic Church boasts of its visible unity. The Protestant Church cannot boast of its unity and in fact the disunity in the Protestant Church is a major factor for the poor health of the Protestant Church. Jesus prayed for his disciples in John 17:20 (He is referring to all believers) that unity might prevail and that it could be noticed by a watching world. I take note of a strange paradox. The unity of the Roman Catholic Church is secured by parochialism and the disunity in the Protestant Church is severed by universalism.

The Roman Catholic Church speaks of a militant and a triumphant church. The militant church is engaged in war against the spiritual forces of darkness. It is the church on earth. The triumphant church is the church in heaven. The Protestant Church must not forget these significant dimensions of the church.

The catholicity and the unity of the visible church are grounded in its common confession by each of its representative members. The Bible teaches that during the days of the Apostles "the Lord was adding to their number day by day" (Acts 2:47) and "the churches were being strengthened in the faith, and were increasing in number daily" (Acts 16:5). Such was the description of the church visible during the days of the Apostles and it is the description of the visible church in our days.

The universal visible church may be further defined as a number of local particular visible churches that join together for collective mutual fellowship. A particular church is a local body of believers who gather to live out their purpose which is to worship God. They also participate in the mission and ministry of the church.

The New Testament speaks of particular churches as they began throughout Asia Minor and Europe. The Churches at Rome, Ephesus, Philippi, et al. were particular churches. There were doctrinal disputes among these local particular churches. However, they did endeavor to maintain doctrinal purity and unity of worship. The universal church has no geographical limits, but it does have ecclesiastical limits. The administration of church government is carried out by elders of the church. However, the government of a particular church ought not to be disenfranchised from the larger church. The visible universal church will do well to acknowledge the catholic as well as the parochial dimension of the church.

When the 16th century Reformation began, the parochialism of Rome was replaced by evangelicalism which is truly universal. While the church was liberated from parochialism, there was the sacrifice of unity for diversity. Our Reformation forefathers used the Latin phrase *unio mystica* (mystical union) to explain *unio cum Christo* (union with Christ). The logical order for the believer is first union with Christ and then communion with Christ. The spiritual union with Christ is applicable to the invisible church in glory, but by His grace the elect exhibit the outward characteristics of the inward change as members of the local particular visible church. The inward change of the individual should reflect outward unity in the church.

The seed of individualism was planted during the 16th century Reformation, but it has taken Satan several centuries to bring about the divisiveness and schism that we see in the visible church today. Division is not necessary, but it follows

3. Nature of the Church

from the sinful human nature. The more sin abounds, the more probable that division will abound. The sad commentary to this important doctrine is that most of the division results from personality conflicts. The challenge for all Christians is to remove the ungodly attitudes that have infiltrated the church. The unity of the church is difficult to maintain when local particular churches are disenfranchised from each other. The complexity of unity in a world of diversity and relativism is not foreign to the church. Paul makes it clear that "we were all baptized into one body - whether Jews or Greeks, whether slaves or free. . ." (1 Corinthians 12:13). However, the apostle also said, "Hold fast the pattern of sound words which you have heard from me" (2 Timothy 1:13). Individual Christians are all members of one body and that one body has one system of doctrine. The "same divine truths" do not allow for a church fragmented into thousands of pieces. John Calvin has rightly said "We...desire nothing else than unity, and whose only bond of union is the eternal truth of God . . ." (*Necessity of Reforming the Church*, by John Calvin).

Unity is not based on feelings, desires, or the spirit of relativism. Unity is based on truth. Christians must not be deceived by the devil to believe that two opposing doctrines can both be right at the same time in the same relationship. False unity will destroy the true unity of the church.

The Holy Spirit that dwells in one person is the same Holy Spirit that dwells in another person. The Holy Spirit cannot and does not contradict Himself. The slightest meditation on this concept is sufficient to dispel any confusion. The Holy Spirit would never interpret Scripture in a contradictory way. For instance, the Holy Spirit would not tell one person to interpret Scripture one way and tell another person to interpret it in a contradictory manner. Contradiction is the result of the sin. Christians must remember that the same Spirit dwells in all.

So how must we determine that a particular church is a true church? The Roman Catholic would appeal to apostolic authority through the Vicar of Christ, the head and king of the church. The early Reformers of the 16th century Reformation deduced from Scripture at least two characteristics of the true church. They are the pure preaching of the Word of God and the due administration of the sacraments. These marks will certainly unify the church which consists of the substance of the duty of the church. However, the fragmentation of the visible church does not necessarily mean that individual churches are not true churches. For instance a particular church may be weakened if it does not properly administer the sacraments, but it still remains a true church. A church may not show its potential strength, if the pure preaching is absent. If the preaching ministry is abused without correction, it will surely lead to heresy and finally apostasy.

The scriptural evidence demands the pure preaching, but none is clearer than Paul's words to Timothy. "Preach the word! Be ready in season and out of season. Convince, rebuke, exhort, with all long-suffering and teaching" (2 Corinthians 2:12-17). The basis for all sound preaching is the Word of God. As John Calvin says, "As soon as men depart, even in the smallest degree from God's Word, they cannot preach anything but falsehoods, vanities, impostures, errors, and deceits."

The sacraments make visible what the Word of God promises. Unfortunately the due administration of the sacraments is not found in many churches. The Bible instructs us to celebrate the Lord's Supper in "sincerity and truth" (1 Corinthians 5:8). Anything less will diminish the true visibility of the church.

4. Purpose of the Church

Oh come, let us worship and bow down; Let us kneel before the LORD our Maker.

Psalm 95:6

Human beings are worshipping creatures. They are aware of the obligation to worship God. There is a driving force built in all human beings that drives them to worship and they love to worship so much that they want to worship as many gods as possible. The biblical doctrine of worship begins with an understanding of the English word "worship". The word "worship" derived from two old English words, "worth" and "ship" deserves special attention. The word "worth" refers to something of value or excellence. "Ship" when used in conjunction with worth is a noun-forming suffix. It often denotes a state, condition, or quality of the noun to which it refers such as friendship or authorship. Biblical worship is the Christian response to God by recognizing and expressing God's worthiness because of His supreme worth. The full counsel of God reveals the primary purpose of the church of God is to worship the triune God.

Sinful man attributes too much worth to himself, which is a form of self-worship. It is also called idolatry or man-made worship. When Paul visited the philosophers at the Areopagus Paul said, "I found an altar with this inscription, 'TO AN UNKNOWN GOD.'" People love to worship man-made things. God will not tolerate self-worship. When Christians invent things to worship, God despises that worship. "I hate, I despise your feast days, and I do not savor your sacred assemblies. Though you offer Me burnt offerings and your grain offerings, I will not accept *them,* nor will I regard your fattened peace offerings. Take away from Me the noise of your songs, for I will not hear the melody of your stringed instruments" (Amos 5:21-23).

Christians must learn to worship and they must teach the next generation to worship the true God the way that pleases Him. Now is the time to restore biblical worship. Christians are worshipping beings, but they must worship according to the desires and commandments of the one and only true and living God. The first four of the Ten Commandments is the basis to understand who, how, and when to worship. Jesus summarized and simplified the biblical doctrine of worship. "God is spirit and those who worship Him must worship in spirit and truth." (John 4:24). Biblical worship is true; therefore the way it is offered to God must be derived from the only true source, the Word of God. Biblical worship is spiritual; therefore, it is a function of the soul.

It seems to me that many professing Christian worshippers are more interested in entertainment for themselves rather than worshipping the Lord God almighty. People love to worship according to their feelings. We live in an age when true worship has been replaced by entertainment of every sort. The application of managerial theory and the psychobabble theories are the great enemies of true biblical worship. Today the focus is on the worshipper rather than the object of worship, the true and living God. Idolatry in the modern evangelical church is rampant. The building where the church meets for worship is a popular object of worship, especially the multi-million dollar buildings. Music, drama presentations, and other performances have become objects of worship. Pastors, denominations, and church dogma are a few of the many idols found in the modern church. Restoring biblical worship ought to be the primary objective of every Christian.

True worship offered to God is either worthy worship or un-worthy worship. Un-worthy worship may mean the object of worship is wrong or may be the wrong attitude

4. Purpose of the Church

toward the object of worship. Worthy worship comes from a true believer. The true object of adoration, praise and worship is the one true and living God. Worthy worship is that worship that God prescribes in His Word. Worthy worship is called Theocentric (God at the center) worship. Christian worship or if you prefer the term biblical worship ought to be offered to God, not to men, women or children. True biblical worship is not meeting someone's need. True biblical worship does not minister to the needs of people. True worship is not people oriented; it is God oriented.

Since worship expresses the worthiness of God, the glory of God is the end of all true Christian worship. If man institutes and regulates worship by the commandments of men, will God take pleasure in the worship? Contrary to popular opinion, God has commanded Christians to worship Him according to His commandments. In an effort to appease God's wrath, false worshippers bring their man-made offerings and forms of worship to their own shame. God hates sin and He hates sinful worship. The Word of God reveals how God despises worship that He has not commanded. The notion that God prescribes certain practices to be part of public collective worship and frowns on other practices is found in the normative history recorded in Leviticus chapter ten. Scripture says Nadab and Abihu, the sons of Aaron, "offered profane fire before the Lord, which He had not commanded them." "He" is God and God said, "By those who come near Me I must be regarded as holy; and before all the people I must be glorified." It is dangerous to offer worship to God that God has not prescribed and His prescription for worship is found in God's Word, not in the mind of sinful man. (See Leviticus 10:1-3).

There is another biblical reference to this principle in Jeremiah. God warned the Old Testament church with these words. "I will pronounce My judgments on them concerning all their wickedness, whereby they have forsaken Me and have offered sacrifices to other gods, and worshiped the works of their own hands" (Jeremiah 1:16). The Lord spoke to the prophet Isaiah and said "Inasmuch as these people draw near with their mouths and honor me with their lips, But have removed their hearts far from Me, and their fear toward Me is taught by the commandment of men" (Isaiah 29:13). Worship is either by the commandment of man, the commandment of God, or a mixture of both. The commandment of man is idolatry and false worship. A mixture of both, man's commandments and God's commandments is syncretism. Solomon is an example of mixing true worship with false worship. (See 1 Kings 11). The people were offering false worship and God said, "I did not command them, nor did it come into My mind that they should do this abomination to cause Judah to sin" (Jeremiah 32:35). There are many practical and seemingly spiritual offerings according to the mind of man, but it is false worship unless it is according to the mind of God.

A simple but plain fact is that all worship is not acceptable to the Lord our God. We cannot glorify God if we attempt to worship Him apart from His specific instructions. The Puritans called it the regulative principle of worship. The Regulative principle of worship simply means that God institutes and regulates worship according to the Word of God. I'm using the standard English dictionary definition for the word "regulate" that means "to control or direct by a rule, principle, method, etc." The regulative principle is a biblical concept. For instance, the moral law is the standard for Christian behavior. Therefore, Scripture regulates Christian behavior. Scripture regulates every aspect of the Christian life and experience.

There are many narrative descriptions of worship in the Old Testament and a less number in the New Testament. My favorite narrative text is found in the book of Jeremiah. "Thus says the Lord: 'Stand in the court of the Lord's house, and speak to all the cities of Judah, which come to worship in the Lord's house, all the words that I command you to speak to

4. Purpose of the Church

them. Do not diminish a word'" (Jeremiah 26:2). This text from Jeremiah records a scene in the life of the Old Testament church that occurred about 2600 years ago. The one thing that the contemporary church has in common with the church of 2600 years ago is worship.

The people of God in the day of Jehoiakim the king of Judah (609-597) came to the Lord's house to worship. When the people gathered to worship, God warned the worshippers: "I will make this house like Shiloh" unless the people turn from their evil ways. The worshippers could not entertain the thought of terminating worship at Jerusalem. The worshippers were outraged and threatened to kill the preacher.

Why did they get mad at the preacher? Apparently, because he said, speaking for God of course, "I (God) will make this house like Shiloh." Why was Shiloh so important? Shiloh became a place of worship for the Old Testament worshippers during the conquest under the direction of Joshua some 850 years before the scene in Jeremiah. Shiloh was the place of worship under the priesthood of Eli and his two wicked sons. After the Philistines captured the Ark of the Lord, Shiloh lost its significance and was eventually destroyed about 1050 B. C.

When Jeremiah said "this place" (the temple in Jerusalem - the place where the worshippers were presently standing) will be like Shiloh, the worshippers were real upset. The preacher was tampering with their church and their worship. Attitudes toward worship have not changed much in the past 2600 years. Today the murmuring might be something like "What do you mean tampering with my church! I was baptized here and I love this building." Another question that comes to mind is, why would God be so harsh toward those people who allegedly came to worship Him? The answer is very simple once we examine the history of worship among the Old Testament worshippers. Isaiah wrote these inspired words before the fall of the Northern Kingdom in 722 BC: "Their land has also been filled with idols; they worship the work of their hands" (Isaiah 2:8). They worship the work of their hands is equal to self-worship.

The modern church should learn from the 16th century Reformers that "men are experts at inventing idols." They studied the Word of God and concluded that "God...cannot endure new modes of worship to be devised...All kinds of worship invented by men...are accursed and detestable." Like the 16th century Reformers, "We must hold that first the spiritual worship of God does not consist in external ceremonies, or any other kind of works whatsoever; and that no worship is legitimate unless it be so framed as to have for its only rule the will of him to whom it is performed. Men allow themselves to devise contrary to his command, he not only repudiates as void, but distinctly condemns" (John Calvin, The Necessity of Reforming the Church). Notice that Calvin says, "Worship is to be ordered according to rule of the one to whom it is performed."

A study of the full counsel of God is necessary to determine the outward expressions of worship. The debate is divided into two categories. The majority of Protestant churches assume the position that all expressions of worship are acceptable unless they are prohibited in Scripture. The minority report is that only the expressions commanded by God are acceptable. Although there are slight variations among the minority, they generally find prayer, offerings, singing Psalms and hymns, reading and preaching of the Word of God, the sacraments, and the benediction are necessary elements in public collective worship. Some churches are more specific. For instance, some churches believe the Westminster Confession of Faith outlines the biblical elements of worship. They are:

    Reading of the Scripture
    Sound preaching

4. Purpose of the Church

Conscionable hearing of the Word
Obedience with understanding, faith, and reverence
Singing of psalms
Administration of sacraments
Religious oaths and vows
Solemn fastings
Thanksgivings upon special occasions
Prayer

    The only way to offer perfect worship is to offer worship to God through the Mediator, the Lord Jesus Christ, by the power of the Holy Spirit.
    The question is often asked, "How does one offer preaching to God." Every part of true worship must be offered to God, or it is not worship. We sing praise to God, we pray to God, and we worship God with tithes and offerings. Worship is an action of the congregation of God's people, not just the pastor. What about preaching? Do Christian worshippers offer the preaching of the Word of God to God or is it offered to the people in the congregation? When it comes time for the sermon, people reach for their pens and paper. Throughout the sermon they are busy taking notes so they can learn more doctrine or get the points of application. Instruction in doctrine comes under the mission and ministry of the church. If the sermon is worship, it must be offered to God. I've heard Christians say, "I want the sermon to meet my needs." Others have said, "The sermon helps me make it through the week." Preaching is an exercise of worship by believers whereby they believe the preaching, affirm the preaching, and offer the preaching to God in worship. There are several scriptural references relative to believers assembled in worship. The people of God in the Old Testament assembled and "worshipped the Lord" while Ezra "read from the book, from the law of God explaining to give the sense so that they understood the reading" (Nehemiah 8:1-8). The people of God

assembled in the Synagogue to worship and preaching was part of the worship (Luke 4:44; Acts 15:21). Those who are being sanctified (believers) gather to worship and proclaim (preach) the name of God (Hebrews 2:11-13).

Another very unpopular, but very true biblical doctrine is that unregenerate (unsaved) human beings can only see the wrath of God. Therefore, they cannot worship God the right way, even though they have the desire to worship – something. God will not accept worship from an unbeliever. Worship to the true and living God was never intended for unbelievers. In fact, true worship should make unbelievers uncomfortable and maybe even outraged to the degree that they'd like to kill the preacher. That actually happened to Jeremiah (Jeremiah 26).

In Scripture God reveals His covenant salvation to His people as well as His covenant law so His people will know how to live. God's covenant relationship becomes real, secular and sacred through true worship. Once we understand who to worship and how to worship, we will find that the joy of worship is to please God. When we come to worship the Lord, we will not want to omit, diminish, or suppress our understanding of the nature and character of God.

It pleases God when we worship in spirit and truth and we should be filled with joy that God is pleased with the worship offered to him. Worship is spiritual and true worship seeks an intimate communion with the triune God. Worship God in His essence. Worship with a knowledge of God and a sense of the immediate presence of God.

Worship is not having a building, vestments or ceremonies. Worshipers who worship God in Spirit and truth do so because God seeks them and they know him. They know what kind of God He is. They know and understand his sovereignty. Evangelism, morality, education, and dozens of other good and necessary biblical disciplines have been distorted by preachers, elders, church leaders, and laymen alike

4. Purpose of the Church

to the point that theology and especially concepts like the theology of worship are despised.

Worship to the true and living God is intended for believers who find joy in worship according to God's Word so they can see their sin and trust Christ for eternal salvation.

5. Mission and Ministry

THE MISSION OF THE CHURCH

Go therefore and make disciples of all the nations, baptizing them in the name of the Father and of the Son and of the Holy Spirit, teaching them to observe all things that I have commanded you; and lo, I am with you always, even to the end of the age.

Matthew 28:19-20

The purpose of the church is worship (John 4:24; Revelation 14:1-3). God in His wisdom gave the church a mission and ministry to accomplish the purpose of the church. The mission of the church is apostolic. The ministry includes the works of service necessary for the mission.

The Latin word *missio*, from which we get the English word mission, refers to "a sending forth." The Greek word *apostello*, from which we get the word apostle, refers to "one sent by authority of the sender to act on the senders behalf." The gospels and the Acts of the Apostles magnify the apostolic mission of the church (Matthew 28:18-20; John 17:6-18; Acts 13:1-3). The Lord Jesus Christ was sent on a mission and He sends His disciples on a mission. The two dimensions of the mission given by injunction are to make disciples and to teach the Word of God.

Evangelism is part of the process necessary to make disciples. However, instruction for the purpose of conversion is only one aspect of making disciples. Discipleship is an educational process. We are all disciples of one sort of another. A disciple is simply someone who learns from a teacher. In modern times, a disciple is a student. A Christian student is one who learns, believes, and practices the truth. Preaching the whole counsel of God is necessary for the convert to become a student. Christians are students of Jesus Christ by the means appointed by God. The two primary instruments include a curriculum and a teacher. The Bible is the curriculum and elders of the church are the teachers. The student of Jesus Christ through the means appointed must have the ability to receive the truth. Some people are able to receive the truth and some are not able to receive the truth (See John 8:42-47). Discipleship is not mere mental assent to a system of doctrine. The disciple (student) will desire to put the truth into practice.

Evangelism is a world and life view that embraces the good news of God's saving grace and sharing that good news with others. The evangelical church may have lost the biblical doctrine of evangelism to a man designed doctrine of evangelism. A Scottish minister addressed this issue in the 19th century in a sermon to his congregation.

> It will be a sad day for our country if the men, who luxuriate in the excitement of man-made revivals, shall with their one-sided views of truth, which have ever been the germs of serious errors, their lack of spiritual discernment, and their superficial experience, become the leaders of the religious thought and the conductors of religious movements…They may be successful in galvanizing, by a succession of sensational shocks, a multitude of dead, till they seem to be alive, and they raise them from their crypts, to take a place amidst the living in the house of the Lord; but far better would it be to leave the dead in the place of the dead, and prophesy to them there, till the living God himself shall quicken them. For death will soon resume its sway.

It is popular to admit people into the fellowship of the church and to the Lord's Table without any credible profession

5. Mission and Ministry

of faith, any understanding of the teaching of Christ, and no evidence of a true conversion.

It almost seems that some Christians believe and live as if the final purpose of the gospel is evangelization of the world. I do not believe the Bible teaches any such idea. Taking the gospel, that is evangelizing, to a lost world is a duty for all Christians - a duty that must not be ignored on one hand, but on the other hand, evangelization must not become something Christians worship. Jesus said, "You shall be witnesses to Me...to the end of the earth" (Acts 1:8). Announcing the good news to the unbeliever is necessary to fulfill the mission of the church.

The Lord Jesus Christ gave the church elders, with authority, "to teach them (disciples) to observe all that I (Jesus Christ) commanded you" (Matthew 28:20). The mission of the church includes teaching the full counsel of God. To teach the full counsel of God means to teach the Word of God systematically and accurately to every Christian. Teaching the full counsel of God calls Christians to obey the Word of God in faith and practice.

After His resurrection, Jesus appeared to a couple of His disciples. "Then He said to them, 'These are the words which I spoke to you while I was still with you, that all things must be fulfilled which were written in the Law of Moses and the Prophets and the Psalms concerning Me.' And He opened their understanding, that they might comprehend the Scriptures'" (Luke 24:44-45). This is a particularly powerful statement and the only one in the New Testament that mentions Jesus Christ as the focus in all three divisions of the Hebrew Bible. When Jesus spoke those words, He opened their understanding, that they might comprehend the Scriptures.

The composition of the teaching ministry of the church requires four components: The teacher, the student, the Word of God, and the Holy Spirit. If any of those are absent, the teaching ministry will not mature. Furthermore, the Christian will not know how to "observe all things that Christ commanded."

Every Christian is responsible and accountable before God to participate in the mission of the church. The mission should not be confused with the purpose and ministry of the church.

THE MINISTRY OF THE CHURCH

And He Himself gave some to be apostles, some prophets, some evangelists, and some pastors and teachers, for the equipping of the saints for the work of ministry, for the edifying of the body of Christ, till we all come to the unity of the faith and of the knowledge of the Son of God, to a perfect man, to the measure of the stature of the fullness of Christ; that we should no longer be children, tossed to and fro and carried about with every wind of doctrine, by the trickery of men, in the cunning craftiness of deceitful plotting, but, speaking the truth in love, may grow up in all things into Him who is the head—Christ—from whom the whole body, joined and knit together by what every joint supplies, according to the effective working by which every part does its share, causes growth of the body for the edifying of itself in love.

Ephesians 4:11-16

The mission of the church and the ministry of the church complement each other. The ministry of the church begins by "serving the Lord with all humility" (Acts 20:19). The servants of the Lord, (apostles, prophets, evangelists, pastors and teachers), are responsible for "equipping the saints for the work of ministry." The word "ministry" is derived from the word "minister" that literally means "to serve". The ministry of the church consists of serving in the body of Christ. Paul summarizes the ministry in his letter to the Ephesians.

5. Mission and Ministry

Christ gave His church pastors and teachers to prepare God's people for works of service, so the mission of the church will be complete. Elders fill the office of the pastor and teacher. They are responsible for the oversight of the congregation. The Word of God defines this particular office. "The elders who are among you I exhort, I who am a fellow elder and a witness of the sufferings of Christ, and also a partaker of the glory that will be revealed: Shepherd the flock of God which is among you, serving as overseers, not by compulsion but willingly, not for dishonest gain but eagerly; nor as being lords over those entrusted to you, but being examples to the flock" (1 Peter 5:1-4). Pastors ought to have the gift of preaching and teaching. If the pastor has been faithful in his preparation, he ought to be able and willing to teach other pastors. Paul explains this concept to Timothy. "If you instruct the brethren in these things, you will be a good minister of Jesus Christ, nourished in the words of faith and of the good doctrine which you have carefully followed" (1 Timothy 4:6).

The role of the pastor is one of spiritual oversight. The role of the teacher is one skilled, able, and willing to teach the "good doctrine." There are two roles, but one office, the office of elder. The office of elder has taken a turn for the worse in recent centuries among evangelicals. The office holders have compromised their office, which will eventually cause the elder to abandon his biblical role.

I've studied and observed pastoral roles for nearly thirty years and conclude that the primary cause of the biblical pastor's disappearance is modernity. Modernity is a system produced by modernization and development. Modernity ultimately embraces relativism as the standard to interpret all of life. Since modernity has been a prevailing cultural philosophy, the roles of pastor and teacher take on worldviews occupied by the modern mind. In simple terminology, it is GIGO (garbage in – garbage out). This term was coined to explain how data input in a computer would ultimately be reflected in the output. If bad doctrine goes in, bad doctrine comes out. If good doctrine goes in, good doctrine comes out.

The pastor/teacher in the past was a church doctor, skilled in metaphysics, and the theologian in residence. His world and life view was rooted in the Word of God, not the words of men. There was a time when the pastor was truly a minister. Now the modern pastor is a CEO, a therapeutic counselor, and a management expert. There was a time when the pastor/teacher was educated in the classics, understood the historical philosophy of the culture, and respected in the community. Even though many hold a degree, they are uneducated and held in suspect by the world around them. The pastor/teacher was once a man of truth; now an irrational guru.

The pastors and teachers are the foundation for the ministry of the church, but the whole church must serve to build up the body of Christ. The pastors and teachers have the responsibility to prepare the saints for the mission and ministry of the church. Every Christian must be involved in the ministry of the church according to the gift Christ has given him or her. The elders of the church must identify the gifts of every individual. Then the elder's duty is to strengthen the gift in that person so the ministry will be complete. The perfection of the ministry of the church will be in the New Heavens and the New Earth.

Paul explains the tactics of the enemy that prevent the saints from participating in the ministry of the church. Paul says, "we should no longer be children, tossed to and fro and carried about with every wind of doctrine, by the trickery of men, in the cunning craftiness of deceitful plotting" (Ephesians 4:14). Avoid the tactics of the enemy and embrace the instruction from the Master by "speaking the truth in love" (Ephesians 4:15).

Is it possible that some particular churches have lost the ministry of the church? Is the foundation cracked and unstable? Have the gifts been absconded by the enemy? If so, then

5. Mission and Ministry

we should pray for the grace of repentance and recover the biblical ministry of the church.

6. Invite Unbelievers to Church

Now after John was put in prison, Jesus came to Galilee, preaching the gospel of the kingdom of God, and saying, "The time is fulfilled, and the kingdom of God is at hand. Repent, and believe in the gospel.
Mark 1:14-15

"I'm going to church this Sunday," says Mr. Devout Christian. Mrs. Devout Christian saw her friend in the store and said, "We'd love to have you come to church this Sunday." Sometimes Christians say, "Come visit our church." These comments about the church come from religious jargon inherited from previous generations. Everyone from Sunday School children to trained theologians use terminology about the church that is not biblically consistent.

The church on earth consists of professing Christians. They profess faith in Christ and believe the basic doctrine of Holy Scripture. However, many professing Christians fail to understand the biblical doctrine of "the church." The church is not a building, a campus, or a place. It is the people who belong to God through faith in Jesus Christ by the power of the Holy Spirit. To invite someone to church means they are invited to profess faith in Christ and believe the basic doctrine of Holy Scripture by the power of the Holy Spirit. Actually, inviting someone to church is part of the mission of the church, commonly known as evangelism.

Christian evangelism is part of the Christian worldview. Many questions have been asked about evangelism. What is the message of evangelism? What is the right method of evangelism? What is the goal of evangelism? Where is the mandate for evangelism? Although every question is important, Christians must first be certain that the concept of evangelism is a discipline in Christian theology. Evangelism is not the purpose of the church. The purpose of the church is to worship God. Evangelism comes under the mission and ministry of the church. There is a curious notion among many evangelicals that the primary duty of the church is evangelism.

I must admit that early in my Christian life I thought I contributed something to God's effort to save me. Maybe it was the sinners prayer or going to the front of a church during the alter call or at the very least I exercised my faith. Pride was the problem. After my conversion, my goal was to win people to Jesus. During those early years, I prayed with several dozen people to receive Christ. As far as I can judge, only one of them ever made a serious commitment to worship the Lord. After a serious and searching inquiry into the Word of God, it became abundantly clear that I could not do anything to save myself or anyone else. I pray that my misguided evangelistic efforts have not deceived anyone into believing they are Christians when they are not Christians at all. I studied the Bible and learned the holiness of God in contrast to my sinfulness. The good news was that I was declared righteous because of the sacrifice of Jesus Christ. The Holy Spirit enabled me to believe the gospel of kingdom of Jesus Christ. I began to make some headway toward understanding biblical evangelism. If people do not understand God's law and His judgment, they will not be convicted of their sin nature or their sinful acts. If they are not convicted of their sin, they will have no need to hear and understand the gospel.

The word "gospel" literally means, "to announce good tidings or good news." It often refers to the good news of God's saving grace. The "evangel" is the good news of the message of the redemptive work of Christ. When we add "ism" then we adopt as a world and life view the salvation message of Jesus Christ. Therefore, evangelism is the way of life for Christians.

The evangelistic enterprise begins with a "seeker." All people "should seek the Lord in the hope that they might

6. Invite Unbelievers to Church

grope for Him and find Him..." (Acts 17:27). To "grope" for the Lord implies that one is searching for something. The unbeliever attempts to find relief from the guilt of sin. The believer has a duty to make the following announcement: "Repent, and believe the gospel" (Mark 1:15). The method of evangelism used by the early evangelical church may be described as the doctrine of seeking. It was the method used by many of the English and early American Puritans, especially by the great evangelist Jonathan Edwards.

Who is responsible for the work of evangelism? In the New Testament, all Christians were involved in the task of evangelism (Acts 8:4-5). Ordained ministers and layman proclaim the gospel. Those called by God to the ministry of the Word have a primary responsibility to "do the work of an evangelist." However, every Christian has the responsibility to evangelize others. Christians evangelize by what they say and how they live in a fallen world. God is the Evangelist par excellence. He gave us the evangel and He gives us the opportunity to present the evangel, but He alone can grant new life.

John Calvin, probably one of the first notable Protestant missionaries and evangelists said, "How joyful we must be when the reign of the Son of God...multiplies and when the good seed of His doctrine is scattered abroad. . . . However, you should be mindful that wherever we go, the Cross of Jesus Christ will follow us."

Jonathan Edwards left the church with a legacy that has almost been forgotten. The legacy was a biblical view of evangelism, a God-centered evangelism known as seeking. Unfortunately, many evangelistic messages are man-centered and that discourages the seeking doctrine. Man-centered evangelism believes that an unconverted sinner can cause God to change the sinner's heart. Its message is the unbiblical message that God certainly helps in the process of salvation, but ultimately man must save himself. Jonathan Edwards took the view that God could cause the heart to be changed and then the converted sinner could believe.

Jonathan Edwards on his remarks "Concerning Efficacious Grace" wrote, "It is manifest that the Scripture supposes, that if ever men are turned from sin, God must undertake it, and he must be the doer of it; that it is his doing that must determine the matter..." (*Works of Jonathan Edwards*, Hickman ed., Volume 2, page 543). As you can see Edwards believed that God acted to renew the will of which the individual could not cause the will to change. Only God the Holy Spirit could cause the will to change so that the sinner could believe and repent. This is commonly called "being born again."

Later in the same treatise Edwards says, "In efficacious grace we are not merely passive, nor yet does God do some and we do the rest. However, God does all, and we do all. God produces all, and we act all. For that is what he produces, viz. our own acts. God is the only proper author and fountain; we only are the proper actors. . . ." You can see that Edwards believed that man acted because of God's doing. The difference, on this issue, between Jonathan Edwards and Billy Graham is that Dr. Graham believes that man can do something, which will cause God to act. One reference in Scripture is sufficient to see who does what. "And a certain woman named Lydia, from the city of Thyatira, a seller of purple fabrics, a worshiper of God, was listening; and the Lord opened her heart to respond to the things spoken by Paul" (Acts 16:14). Read it slowly and notice who did what to make who believe what. It was not the gospel message that changed the heart of Lydia. It was not Lydia's faith that changed her heart. It was not a sinner's prayer that changed her heart. The Lord changed her heart, so that Lydia could believe the gospel. In addition, notice that she was "seeking" God before the Lord changed her heart.

6. Invite Unbelievers to Church

Although using doctrinal name tags is often considered offensive, it is necessary for classification. Arminian evangelism refers to the man-centered evangelism. Calvinistic evangelism refers to the God-centered evangelism. The reasons for an affinity to Arminian evangelism are many. Arminianism was popularized in America by Charles Finney and his followers. Based on my thirty years of experience in the evangelical church the overwhelming majority of Christians believe and practice Arminian evangelism. It is called man-centered evangelism because it makes man the cause of salvation. Arminian evangelism teaches that the unconverted sinner is able to believe and repent before the Holy Spirit changes the heart. Regeneration (the proper word for born again) takes place because the sinner believes.

Calvinistic evangelism teaches that man is not able to believe until God regenerates the heart. Arminianism teaches that "God, as far as he is concerned, wished to bestow equally upon all people the benefits which are gained by Christ's death; but that the distinction by which some rather than others come to share in the forgiveness of sins and eternal life depends on their own free choice. . ." (*Canons of Dort*, Second Main Point of Doctrine, Section VI). Calvinism teaches that "the fact that some receive from God the gift of faith within time, and that others do not, stems from his eternal decision" (*The Canons of Dort*, The First Main Point of Doctrine, Article 6). Arminians teach that man makes the decision (often called the sinners prayer or some other pragmatic, but unbiblical tool). Calvinism teaches that God makes the decision. Arminianism teaches that "unregenerate man is not strictly or totally dead in his sins or deprived of all capacity for spiritual good but is able to hunger and thirst for righteousness or life and to offer the sacrifice of a broken and contrite spirit which is pleasing to God" (*Canons of Dort*, The Third and Fourth Main Points of Doctrine, Section IV). Calvinism teaches that "all people are conceived in sin and are born children of wrath, unfit for any saving good, inclined to evil, dead in their sins, and slaves to sin; without the grace of the regenerating Holy Spirit they are neither willing nor able to return to God, to reform their distorted nature, or even to dispose themselves to such reform" (*Canons of Dort*, The Third and Fourth Main Points of Doctrine, Article 3). If men are dead in sin and not willing to return to God, then nothing that person can say, do, or think will cause his or her salvation. Just as Rome errs with baptismal regeneration, evangelicals err with decisional regeneration.

The reasons for so much deviant evangelistic activity among evangelicals are too many and too complicated for the purpose of this brief manuscript. However, the fundamental cause of so much error in evangelistic endeavors in our day can be traced to some of the Bible institutes, Christian liberal arts colleges, Bible colleges, seminaries and other training centers for Christian workers. These institutions not only err by teaching unbiblical evangelistic doctrine and practice, they propagate the idea that evangelism is the primary duty of Christians. When a young Christian develops a passion for some aspect of religion, it is difficult to re-channel those passions in another direction. These institutions seem to overlook the more important mandate - the mandate to worship God. If we search the Scriptures carefully and diligently, we will learn that worship is the predominant mandate throughout the Old Testament and the New Testament. We will not only learn that we must worship God, we will learn how to worship Him.

The Arminian approach to evangelism encourages people to join the church who may be unconverted. How terrible to lead people to think they may be converted when they may or may not be converted. New converts ought to be introduced to the basic doctrine of Christianity and taught the purpose, mission and ministry of the church.

6. Invite Unbelievers to Church

Baptism, praying at the altar in a church, praying "the sinner's prayer" or any other activity on the part of an unconverted sinner will not produce salvation. God and God alone can enable the person to repent and believe. When we command someone to "believe on the Lord Jesus Christ", we must remember that there is a contingency which is a work of the Lord. A person might repent and believe many things about the Lord Jesus Christ, but until God creates a new heart in him or her, salvation is not possible. Nevertheless, encourage everyone to seek the Lord while He may be found. Then ask the unconverted sinner to believe on the Lord Jesus and receive and rest in Him as Lord and Savior.

So what must the evangelist do so that the unconverted sinner will seek God? Tell him or her to read the Bible and to attend Bible studies. Explain the law and the gospel. Tell him or her to seek the Lord while He may be found. They can seek the Lord by being present for the preaching and teaching of the Word of God, obey His commandments, and ask God's people to pray for his or her conversion. Now I can imagine someone may say, "You will not get many church members that way." True! However, is the goal to get church members or is it to obey everything that Christ has commanded?

God created us to worship Him. Invite unbelievers to church; then invite the church to worship, Bible study, prayer and fellowship. We cannot worship the Lord unless we love Him and obey His commandments. One commandment out of hundreds of His commandments is to "Make disciples of all nations . . . teaching them to observe all that I commanded you. . . ." (Matthew 28:19-20). To put it another way invite unbelievers into the true church. If the unbeliever professes faith, then disciple him or her with the basic doctrine of Scripture. It will reflect your love for God and His church.

There is no need to invite believers to church, because they are the church. Invite unbelievers into the church.

7. Invite Believers to Worship

God is Spirit, and those who worship Him must worship in spirit and truth.

John 4:24

The church has the great privilege to assemble for worship. It is not only a privilege to assemble for worship; it is a commandment. In the previous chapter I explained the need to invite unbelievers into the church. When the unbeliever is converted he or she becomes one of the many among God's church on earth. It is nonsense to invite a believer to church, since he or she is part of it. The believer and other members of the household of God assemble to worship, study God's Word, fellowship and pray. This chapter focuses on the preaching ministry of the church and the administration of the Sacraments, both of which are elements of worship.

There are hundreds of commandments in the Bible. Some of them are positive (do such and such) and some are negative (do not do such and such). The history of the church attests to the reformations that lead to revivals. In every case, the reformation (the discovery or re-discovery of biblical truth) required a renewed commitment to biblical authority. Citizens of the heavenly kingdom are responsible to obey all God's commandments no matter how many and no matter how difficult they may seem. One commandment to the church is to "preach the word" (2 Timothy 4:1). There is another commandment that is largely ignored in the church today: "do this in remembrance of me" (Luke 22:19 and 1 Corinthians 11:24). God's means of grace are several, but two aspects of His means of grace are particularly identified as ordinances that are reserved for the ministry of the church. They are the Word and the Sacraments. Our understanding of God's means of grace will have its effect upon those who gather to worship the true and living God.

The preaching and teaching ministry will be one of the primary means to accomplish the mission and ministry of the church. Unfortunately, a generation of Christians who are taught unbiblical doctrine can produce a generation of Christians who could cause serious calamity in the church. On the other hand a generation of Christians who are taught the full counsel of God may cause a revival in the church.

Doctrinal preaching and teaching assume the role of education. Paul said that we are instructed to receive the Lord Jesus and live a holy life. The key word is instruction. People need proper instruction to understand the gospel and then they need proper instruction to live the Christ-like life. It is not enough to know the laws of God in nature and revelation, but Christians must discipline their mind, emotions, and will to work in harmony with these laws.

It is important to remember that doctrine will precede practice, so correct doctrine is essential for the Christian. The apostle Paul must have been concerned about doctrinal preaching and teaching since he devoted a major part of his writing to Timothy about the subject. Should Christians today be any less concerned?

In the Old Testament a watchman may serve in one of several capacities. Watchmen were stationed on city walls so they could alert the city if hostile action threatened the city. Watchmen were also appointed to watch over fields and vineyards during the time of harvest.

The prophets used the term "watchman" as an allegorical device to describe a prophet as a watchman for God. It was the duty of the watchman to announce to the people of God either good news or impending doom.

God commissioned the prophet Ezekiel to serve as a watchman for the house of Israel. (See and read Ezekiel 33:1-11). Interestingly enough Ezekiel had already been taken

7. Invite Believers to Worship

captive to Babylon and apparently ministered to a group of Jewish captives by the River Chebar. You might call them the underground church of the Old Testament. Ezekiel spoke words of hope concerning the restoration of the Old Testament saints to the land of their forefathers. Ezekiel also spoke words of judgment to the Old Testament saints in exile. His warning was turn to the Lord, because God delighted in those who turned from sin.

Ezekiel's words are as fresh as this morning's newspaper and we need to hear afresh the Word of God delivered from the mouthpiece of God. The mouthpiece of God must announce to the people of God the law and the gospel for their own spiritual nurture and growth. The evangelical church is at a point of crisis. All too often the shepherds are slumbering and not watching for the wolves as they subtly separate the flock by their charm and false doctrine.

The necessity imposed on ministers to proclaim the whole counsel of God is not to be taken lightly by the pastor or the congregation. If the preacher neglects to preach the whole counsel of God and does not warn the congregation, then the congregation will perish.

> I have made you a watchman for the house of Israel; therefore you shall hear a word from My mouth and warn them for Me. When I say to the wicked, 'O wicked man, you shall surely die!' and you do not speak to warn the wicked from his way, that wicked man shall die in his iniquity; but his blood I will require at your hand. (Ezekiel 33:7-8)

If the preacher neglects God's mandate, the minister himself will be dealt with as the author of that sinner's destruction. The responsibility placed on the watchman is a profound obligation. I cannot stress enough the emphasis that

God places on the preaching of the Word. The examples from Scripture are not very pleasing to the ear.

> If any man is preaching to you a gospel contrary to that which you received, let him be accursed. (Galatians 1:9)

> Some to be sure, are preaching Christ even from envy and strife, but some also from good will. (Philippians 1:15)

> Furthermore, when I came to Troas to preach Christ's gospel, and a door was opened to me by the Lord, I had no rest in my spirit, because I did not find Titus my brother; but taking my leave of them, I departed for Macedonia. Now thanks be to God who always leads us in triumph in Christ, and through us diffuses the fragrance of His knowledge in every place. For we are to God the fragrance of Christ among those who are being saved and among those who are perishing. To the one we are the aroma of death leading to death, and to the other the aroma of life leading to life. And who is sufficient for these things? For we are not, as so many, peddling the word of God; but as of sincerity, but as from God, we speak in the sight of God in Christ. (2 Corinthians 2:12-17)

Paul's scathing analysis of false preachers ought to bring fear to the soul of any man preparing to preach a sermon. Too much preaching today is fake; false preachers are "peddling" the Word of God. Preaching the Word of God has a fragrance. To some it smells bad and to others it smells good. Sound preaching from the Word of God is a good aroma to God. Fake preaching is a stench to His nostrils, because it is derived from unbiblical doctrine.

7. Invite Believers to Worship

How must God's mouthpiece speak to God's people? "I have made you a watchman for the house of Israel; therefore you shall hear a word from My mouth and warn them for Me" (Ezekiel 33:11).

God's mouthpiece, Ezekiel, received his words directly from God by inspiration. Today God's mouthpiece, the preacher, must consult the Word of God that was given by inspiration to know how to speak God's words. The only way a preacher can preach sound doctrine is to consult the Word of God. Unfortunately there are many preachers today who consult the enticing words of man's wisdom to preach the Word of God. Preaching and teaching the Word of God must not be intermingled with "persuasive words of human wisdom" so says the apostle Paul and he goes on to say that preaching must be of the Spirit and of power, that your faith should not be in the wisdom of men but in the power of God.

The pastors that are called to labor in the ministry of the Word are to preach sound doctrine. Paul explained this doctrine to Timothy. "Hold fast the pattern of sound words which you have heard from me…" (2 Timothy 1:13).

The pew has the duty to hear the preacher. How must God's mouthpiece, the preacher, be heard by God's people, the pew? "Whoever hears the sound of the trumpet and does not take warning, if the sword comes and takes him away his blood shall be on his own head. He heard the sound of the trumpet, but did not take warning" (Ezekiel 33:4-5).

The trumpet allegorically represents the Word of God. The law and the gospel of God's grace constitute the Word of God. The law is needed to show man his sin and the gospel is needed to save man from his sin.

The function of the Hebrew verb "shama" translated "he heard" may be either a completed action or an instantaneous action. The context makes me believe that the sound was instantaneously impressive and even startling.

The *Westminster Larger Catechism* question number 160 is thought provoking. The question, "What is required of those that hear the Word preached?" may be summarized as follows. They must:

> Attend upon the preaching with diligence.
> Prepare for the preaching of the word of God.
> Attend the preaching prayerfully.
> Examine what they hear by the Scriptures.
> Receive the truth with faith, love, and meekness.
> Receive the truth with readiness of mind.
> Meditate and confer upon the preaching.
> Hide the preaching in their hearts.
> Bring forth the fruit of the preaching in their lives.

The minister is appointed by God to watch over the souls committed to his charge. If he faithfully and fearfully fulfills his responsibility as a mouthpiece for God, then God's people are obligated to receive and take pleasure in the doctrine of the true and living God. God's watchmen must be prepared to be God's mouthpiece. God's mouthpiece must have a passion for the Word of God and those who hear from God must have a passion to be reformed by the Word of God. Do you have that passion?

The preaching of the Word of God may convict you of sin in your life and that is good. However, the preaching of the Word of God will build you up and strengthen you to serve God.

Although God has chosen several ways to communicate His grace to His church, He primarily uses the Word and the Sacraments as a means of grace. Somehow or another the reading and preaching of the Word of God has survived and remains considerably stronger than the proper administration of the sacraments. The apostle Paul says "Christ our Passover also has been sacrificed. Therefore let us celebrate the feast

7. Invite Believers to Worship

with the unleavened bread of sincerity and truth" (1 Corinthians 5:8). Just a little consideration and inquiry should provoke us to ask the question: Do we celebrate and participate in the Lords Supper in sincerity and truth?

My acquaintance with the many evangelical churches does not leave me with the impression that they are celebrating and participating in the sacrament of the Lord's Supper with any deep sense of sincerity and truth. In fact, it seems that the tradition of men dictates the doctrine of the Sacrament of the Lord's Supper. If men are important then let us consider the doctrine of the Lord's Supper from the mouths of men.

Justin Martyr (100 - 165 A.D.) wrote a defense of the Christian religion, which he called his "First Apology". In this document, we have an account of a worship service.

> On the day called Sunday there is a meeting in one place of those who live in cities or the country, and memoirs of the apostles or the writings of the prophets are read as long as time permits. When the reader has finished, the president in a discourse urges and invites [us] to the imitation of these noble things. Then we all stand up together and offer prayers. And, as said before, when we have finished the prayer, bread is brought, and wine and water, and the president similarly sends up prayers and thanksgivings to the best of his ability, and the congregation assents, saying the Amen; the distribution, and reception of the consecrated [elements] by each one, takes place and they are sent to the absent by the deacons. (*Early Christian Fathers*, p. 287)

During the severe persecution by the Roman Empire in the 2nd and 3rd centuries an African theologian named Tertullian indicates that the Sacrament of the Lord's Supper was a part of the "assemblies before day break." From the

Apostolic Tradition of Hippolytus we find that the order of worship included the Lord's Supper at every meeting (*Documents of the Christian Church*, p. 76). The preponderance of evidence indicates that the early church celebrated and participated in the Lord's Supper each week.

These early church fathers lived close in time to the life and actions of the Apostles. Although the early church fathers were acquainted with some of the Apostles, they were still subject to err. However, we cannot completely ignore their teaching if they have correctly interpreted Scripture.

Some of the 16th century Reformers attempted to restore the Lord's Supper to its rightful place as a Sacrament after it had been abused for centuries by the Church of Rome. John Calvin saw the corruption that had taken place and he wrote vigorously to recover the correct doctrine and practice of the Lord's Supper in the Protestant church. He realized that "whatever benefit may come to us from the Supper requires the Word: whether we are to be confirmed in faith, or exercised in confession, or aroused to duty, there is need of preaching" (*Institutes of the Christian Religion*, 4.17.39). We are to receive the Lord's Supper with "faith and thankfulness of heart, and, inasmuch as we are not so of ourselves, by his mercy make us worthy of such a feast" (*Institutes of the Christian Religion*, 4.17.43). If the Lord Himself makes us worthy to receive the sacred meal, then how often should we show our "faith and thankfulness"? The logic and meaning of the language (i.e. if we have faith and if we are thankful) should drive us to the Lord's Table immediately and often. Calvin believed that holy men should "retain and protect the frequent practice of communion [as we received it from the apostles]. For they saw that it was most wholesome for believers but that it gradually fell into disuse out of common neglect" (*Institutes of the Christian Religion*, 4.17.45). His doctrine of the Lord's Supper may be summarized in his own words.

7. Invite Believers to Worship

> It was ordained to be frequently used among all Christians in order that they might frequently return in memory to Christ's Passion, by such remembrance to sustain and strengthen their faith, and urge themselves to sing thanksgiving to God and to proclaim his goodness; finally, by it to nourish mutual love, and among themselves give witness to this love, and discern its bond in the unity of Christ's body. For as often as we partake of the symbol of the Lord's body, as a token given and received, we reciprocally bind ourselves to all the duties of love in order that none of us may permit anything that can harm our brother, or overlook anything that can help him where necessity demands and ability suffices. Luke relates in the Acts that this was the practice of the apostolic church, when he says that believers continued in the apostles' teaching and fellowship, in the breaking of bread and in prayers' [Acts. 2:42, cf. Vg.]. Thus, it became the unvarying rule that no meeting of the church should take place without the Word, prayers, partaking of the Supper, and almsgiving. That this was the established order among the Corinthians also, we can safely infer from Paul [cf. 1 Cor. 11:20]. And it remained in use for many centuries after. (*Institutes of the Christian Religion*, 4.17.44)

You will notice that Calvin uses the word "frequent" frequently. Just how often is frequent to the mind of Calvin? "At least once a week" (Institutes of the Christian Religion, 4.17.43). I have heard it said that once a week is too often. Then how often do we show our "faith and thankfulness"? How often do you want to remember Christ? How often do you desire to participate in the meal of the New Covenant?

Other great theologians are also advocates of the frequent (weekly) administration of the Sacrament of the Lord's Supper. "Edwards [Jonathan] believed in a very serious, regular observance of the Lord's Supper. Like John Calvin, he believed that the Eucharist should be observed publicly each week" (*Rational Biblical Theology*, vol. 3, p. 447).

The *Directory for The Public Worship of God* was adopted by the Westminster assembly. The same men who drafted the Westminster Confession of Faith and Catechisms also left us with their views on the celebration of the Lord's Supper. Their views are closely in line with some of the early church fathers and the early Reformers. Their words are sufficient for the contemporary church. "The Communion, or supper of the Lord, is frequently to be celebrated, but how often, may be considered and determined by the ministers, and other church-governors of each congregation, as they shall find most convenient of the comfort and edification for the people committed to their charge....Where this Sacrament cannot with convenience be frequently administrated, it is requisite that public warning be given the Sabbath-day before the administration thereof." There is no reason to believe these divines wanted God's people to be deprived of a regular (weekly, bi-weekly, monthly, etc) communion, but if because of circumstances it was not possible, public notice should be required.

After all is said and done men like Tertullian, Calvin, Edwards, and the Westminster assembly may be wrong. On the other hand, churches that celebrate the Lord's Supper every three months may be wrong. We must go to Scripture to see who is right and who is wrong.

The Lord Jesus Christ said, "this is my body which is broken for you; do this in remembrance of Me" (Luke 22:19 and 1 Cor. 11:24). Luke and Paul use the Greek word *poieite* to describe the expected action of the verb. This verb means "to do" or "to perform" or "to practice" something. In its context, it means to participate (notice it is participate not celebrate) in the Sacrament of the Lord's Supper. It is a

7. Invite Believers to Worship

present, active, imperative, second person, plural verb. It is an injunction and the obligation to obey this command cannot be altered or ignored. The language certainly allows for repeated and frequent action known as an iterative present verb. Sometimes the present active imperative is connected with the logic of a repeated action (1 Thessalonians 5:17). Some portion of Scripture may seem ambiguous and the morphological and syntactical technicalities may be debated at great length. However, the language in Luke and 1 Corinthians is plain and forthright. Christians must participate in the Sacrament of the Lord's Supper frequently and every three months is not frequent. The language in the book of Acts (as pointed out by Calvin) also points toward a frequent administration of the Lord's Supper.

We are to celebrate the Lord's Supper in "sincerity and truth" (1 Corinthians 5:8). Is it possible to participate and celebrate the Sacrament of the Lord's Supper in sincerity and truth on an irregular basis? Does the Bible imply an infrequent administration (every two or three months)? On the other hand, does it favor a more frequent administration? What does Scripture teach?

There is a great emphasis today among many churches to bring drama and skits into worship services. All such ideas are foreign to Holy Scripture, but the Sacrament of the Lord's Supper is a mandate. The Lord's Supper is drama inspired by the Word of God. We will do well to obey the Lord by consistently, faithfully, thankfully, sincerely, truthfully, and regularly celebrate and participate in the Sacrament of the Lord's Supper.

8. Why?

Then He said to His disciples, "Therefore I say to you, do not worry about your life, what you will eat; nor about the body, what you will put on. Life is more than food, and the body is more than clothing. Consider the ravens, for they neither sow nor reap, which have neither storehouse nor barn; and God feeds them. Of how much more value are you than the birds? And which of you by worrying can add one cubit to his stature? If you then are not able to do the least, why are you anxious for the rest? Consider the lilies, how they grow: they neither toil nor spin; and yet I say to you, even Solomon in all his glory was not arrayed like one of these. If then God so clothes the grass, which today is in the field and tomorrow is thrown into the oven, how much more will He clothe you, O you of little faith?

"And do not seek what you should eat or what you should drink, nor have an anxious mind. For all these things the nations of the world seek after, and your Father knows that you need these things. But seek the kingdom of God, and all these things shall be added to you. "Do not fear, little flock, for it is your Father's good pleasure to give you the kingdom. Sell what you have and give alms; provide yourselves money bags which do not grow old, a treasure in the heavens that does not fail, where no thief approaches nor moth destroys. For where your treasure is, there your heart will be also.

Luke 12:22-34

John Walton is the father on the popular TV series "The Walton's." It is the story of a family living during the Great Depression. On one of the shows he was distressed by his financial condition because of the depression and discouraged because of his lack of control over the present dilemma. He was talking to his wife and said, "I'm not getting any smarter or any richer, I'm just getting older." John Walton is not particularly committed to any religious belief and he is not a philosopher. He is just an average man looking in the face of toil and trouble, but asking a very religious and philosophical question – "why?" I have two questions to examine. Why worry about anything? However why not ask the question "why"?

Why do we think the way we think? Why do we do what we do? We think the way we think, because of our essential disposition and inclinations, our innate capacity, and our sensuous contact with the world around us. We may understand these truisms and yet fail to apply them when we ask the question –"why?"

To ask "why" often implies that we are questioning God's generous providence. The word providence is a word used in theology to describe God's provision for His creation. The Son of God who was present at the creation of this world explained to His disciples how the providence of God gives confidence and hope for every generation.

Jonathan Edwards wrote one of his friends. "As to my circumstance, I still meet with trouble, and expect no other, as long as I live in this world....Let us then endeavor to help one another, though at great distance, in traveling through this wide wilderness; that we may have the more joyful meeting in the land of rest, when we have finished our weary pilgrimage" (*Rational Biblical Theology*, volume 2, page 300). Edwards said a mouthful when he said "weary pilgrimage." The events in recent history cause people to question the integrity of God. To put it in the common language we hear people say, "Where is God in all this mess."

I'm afraid for many; God is not to be found. Why is that? Because, people are looking for Him in all the wrong places. He is not in Washington D. C., a state capital, or in a slick talking politician. The Bible is abundantly clear that God is not limited to one place or the other. The Bible does speak

8. Why?

often about the God in heaven or the God of heaven such as we find in Ecclesiastes "For God is in heaven and you are on the earth; therefore let your words be few" (Ecclesiastes 5:2).

God is in control from His place. He is preserving and governing all that He created. To put it another way "What God creates, God preserves and what God preserves God also governs." All our lives we've heard the old political propaganda "a government of the people, by the people, and for the people." The form of government in the United States is often defined by the word democracy which means the people rule. To be more definitive it is the mob rules. In biblical terms that is bad thinking.

Divine government is defined by that activity of God whereby He rules all things by His sovereign hand, with purpose, ultimately disposing all things according to the counsel of His will. While we may be frustrated with the social, political, and religious world we live in, we must remember that God is the Governor. Not only is he the Governor, God is the King or to put it another way He is the cosmic monarch. Our sinfulness inclines us to view him like we would an earthly monarch which distorts God's character. Unlike a finite monarch, God rules with a righteous right hand.

Jesus spoke to His disciples about God's provision for their needs in the gospel of Luke (See Luke 12:22-34). Our Lord explained the doctrine of providence to his disciples. They appeared to be anxious about their needs. They were believers, but they, like us still have the remnant of the old sin nature. The disciples like us had not grasped the abundantly evident fact that the providence of God was generous and still is generous. The disciples like us were thinking un-theologically about the doctrine of providence. Un-theological thinkers are those who dismiss God from their thoughts when trying to understand existence and the nature of life.

Our Lord puts theology back into the doctrine of providence by making four negative statements. These statements describe the condition that accompanies the sinful nature. However the Lord includes in each negative statement a remedy for the negative conditions.

> Do not worry about your life
> Do not seek what you should eat or drink
> Do not have an anxious mind
> Do not fear

There are several ways to express negation in the Greek language. Sometimes it is hard to translate from ancient Greek into modern English. You may tell a child not to do something before it starts. For instance, do not eat the candy. You may tell a child to stop doing something that has already begun. For example, stop eating the Candy.

In all four commands it would be correct to say "Stop" what you are doing!

> Stop being anxious
> Stop seeking what you may eat
> Stop being worried
> Stop fearing

The disciples were already anxious, worried and fearful, as we often are, and our Lord wanted them and us to stop it!

The way to stop being anxious is listen, believe, and trust the One who created, saved and provides for you. He said, "Do not worry about your life." The word worry comes from the Greek word *merimnaw*, which is most often translated "anxious" in the English Bible. At the time the word was originally penned by the New Testament writer it referred to "A distraction of mind because of trouble and burdens in daily life which leads to an affectionate dispassion." The Lord's

8. Why?

message is clear. The condition is worry. The remedy is to stop worrying.

The disciples were worrying about their lives. The word "life" in our text reminds us of the whole person, both body and soul. The Bible says "man became a living being" referring to both body and soul (Genesis 2:7). Jesus apparently had the maintenance of the body in mind. Jesus used two analogies from nature to teach us to stop being anxious for our bodily needs. The first analogy from animal life was a bird. If God will take care of the ravens, surely God will take care of you, because God created you in His image. The raven was a bird - a crow – that was considered unclean according to Old Testament Levitical laws. It shows us that God takes care of the depraved in His creation.

The second analogy was from plant life. The Creator said, look at the lilies, their beauty and consistency, without any effort on their part. Even common grass receives its part from God.

These natural analogies tell us that God is in absolute control. There is no need to continue in our anxious state of being. To be anxious is to show a lack of understanding and trust in God's hand of providence. We say we believe, but we say, "why did such and such happen?" Then we must ask the Lord to "increase our faith."

The disciples were sinfully disposed toward seeking provisions. The remedy is stop seeking what you may eat and drink. The Lord did not mince words. "Do not seek what you should eat or what you should drink." Our Lord's second negative command is "do not seek" which essentially means, "do not strive after" or "do not be so deliberate and demanding". Jesus does not mean that we should not work and work hard. Yes, work hard and the fruit of your labor will be God's provision. However, you are not to set your heart on food and drink like the rich fool. You, as a disciple of Christ, must have a different motivation from the unbelieving world.

Stop acting like a self seeking and covetous person, because by so doing you show a lack of confidence in God's promise to provide your needs.

The radical difference between a Christian and an unbeliever is the motivation of the heart. If you have been clothed in the righteous of Jesus Christ you are still a sinner, but you will come to hate the sin nature more and more.

The third condition. Worry is a common malady for many Christians. Anxiety leads to worry. The remedy given by the Lord is stop being worried or literally "do not be held in suspense." Stop being so uptight to the point that you can't think straight. If God is your Father He will take care of you so you may spend your time seeking the kingdom of God.

The final negative command from our Lord is stop fearing. "Do not fear little flock." You have no reason to fear, because it is God's good pleasure to give you the kingdom. Jesus called His disciples a "little flock." Just like a flock of sheep needs a shepherd to guide them and guard them, the church needs someone to guide and guard the congregation. The Lord said his flock was little. I suppose the mega-church leaders think they are far more capable of leading a congregation that the Lord Jesus Christ. I find it virtually impossible for a man, a pastor, to have a shepherd/sheep relationship with thousands of people. Satan will try to convince everyone that the shepherd can hire under shepherds to guide the sheep. The congregation ought to be the pastor's treasure. Jesus said, "For where your treasure is, there you heart will be also." He must know each one and encourage them to self-examination of the soul. He must help them see their sin so they will see the need for God's grace. He must know them well enough to remind them privately that their good moral intentions are worthless without a right heart. The pastor must be available to say, face to face, "do not fear."

We are a society of people who have been trained by the world to fret and worry about the acquisition of money,

8. Why?

fame, popularity, prestige, and power. The message from God to the small poor church is, do not fret and worry. The kingdom belongs to you.

Christians need to stop asking God "why" relative to provisions for this life. However, Christians need to ask "why" in the proper context. Evangelical Christians, to a large extent, have abandoned the "why" question in doctrine and godly wisdom. The "why" question has been replaced with the "how" question. How can we present the gospel to make it more palatable? How can we get people to make deeper commitments? How can we raise more money for ministry? Christian thinkers have shifted from "why" to "how". I'm guilty of that crime and see more and more that confession and repentance is in order. I get so busy "doing things" that I forget the reason why I do them. I need to remember John Walton's philosophy. "I'm not getting any smarter or any richer, I'm just getting older." How we do things is not nearly as important as why we think and practice the way we do.

Why worry more about the body than the soul. Jesus put this in its proper perspective. "And do not fear those who kill the body but cannot kill the soul. But rather fear Him who is able to destroy both soul and body in hell" (Matthew 10:28).

The challenge for Christians is to ask questions and look for answers. Why do we believe what we believe? Why have we abandoned classical Christianity? Why are we depending more on our efforts than on the hand of a sovereign God? The answers will not come easy. As it was in the day of Nehemiah, so it is today. "The work is great and extensive" (Nehemiah 4:19).

9. Natural Man

And I, brethren, when I came to you, did not come with excellence of speech or of wisdom declaring to you the testimony of God. For I determined not to know anything among you except Jesus Christ and Him crucified. I was with you in weakness, in fear, and in much trembling. And my speech and my preaching were not with persuasive words of human wisdom, but in demonstration of the Spirit and of power, that your faith should not be in the wisdom of men but in the power of God. However, we speak wisdom among those who are mature, yet not the wisdom of this age, nor of the rulers of this age, who are coming to nothing. But we speak the wisdom of God in a mystery, the hidden wisdom which God ordained before the ages for our glory, which none of the rulers of this age knew; for had they known, they would not have crucified the Lord of glory. But as it is written:

*"Eye has not seen, nor ear heard,
Nor have entered into the heart of man
The things which God has prepared for those who love Him."*

But God has revealed them to us through His Spirit. For the Spirit searches all things, yes, the deep things of God. For what man knows the things of a man except the spirit of the man which is in him? Even so no one knows the things of God except the Spirit of God. Now we have received, not the spirit of the world, but the Spirit who is from God, that we might know the things that have been freely given to us by God. These things we also speak, not in words which man's wisdom teaches but which the Holy Spirit teaches, comparing spiritual things with spiritual. But the natural man does not receive the things of the Spirit of God, for they are foolishness to him; nor can he know them, because they are spiritually discerned

The Present Truth

1 Cor. 2:1-14

When Philip Hughes made has contribution to the life and works of John Calvin, he made a significant statement about the nature of reformation. Hughes said, "If only we remember that the reformation of His church is the work of God, we will wish to be guided in all things by Him rather than by our limited human understanding, lest we 'bring that which is heavenly into subjection to what is earthly.'"

Living with "limited human understanding" has not been a very popular concept in the past couple of hundred years. The enlightenment project and Rationalism of the 18th century and the scientific method of the 19th and 20th centuries were supposed to have saved the world from limited human understanding.

Those centuries of progress were supposed to have removed mans minority. For example, a minor is one who is incapable of making legally binding decisions, because his or her understanding is limited. So when one comes of age his or her understanding is no longer limited. It was said by the advocates of modernity that man was no longer a minor, but was capable of saving himself.

Do you suppose rationalism and the scientific method are the reasons we have so many brilliant people in the world today? Humanity has not been restored. Ignorance abounds as skepticism prevails. Inconsistent and fallacious reasoning is rampant. The modern man in the postmodern western world, saturated with industrialism and technology, is not happier today than he was 300 years ago. In fact the most part of the enlightened modern world is topsy turvey.

Now postmodern man has emerged to save us from the modern man. The postmodern man says there is no such thing as absolute truth. The postmodern interpretive theory is simple. "All you have to do is redefine your terms." It's all in the metanarrative.

9. Natural Man

In a popular academic work by Steven Conner there is a quote by a postmodern liberal named Michael Ryan. He said:

> Rather than being expressive representations of a substance taken to be prior, cultural signs become instead active agents in themselves, creating new substances, new social forms, new ways of acting and thinking, new attitudes, reshuffling the cards of 'fate' and 'nature' and social 'reality'. It is on this margin that culture, seemingly entirely autonomous and detached, turns around and becomes a social and material force, a power of signification that discredits all claims to substantive grounds outside representation and this discrediting applies to political institutions, moral norms, social practices and economic structure. (*Postmodernist culture*, p. 225)

The postmodern culture says God is dead; therefore we have to reshuffle the cards of fate, nature, and reality. The deck of cards according to the postmodern agenda plays out this way; political institutions, moral norms, social practices, and economic structures are signified by our culture and expressed by representatives of that culture. Alasdair MacIntyre, in his book, *After Virtue*, identified the cultural representatives in three categories. They are the manager, therapist, and aesthete. They represent the cultural elites and everyone follows their lead. Managers have authority in public life, therapists have influence in personal life and the aesthete resonates alleged beauty in modern media. These cultural representatives are modern sophists. Their social engineering is deceptive at the root.

The expressions of our cultural dilemma are noticed when it used to be that we heard of adults committing suicide, but now that is a common practice among teenagers. Saving owls is more important than saving babies. Where will it all end?

The reason for all this is that "limited human understanding" cannot satisfy the deepest yearnings in the human soul. The enlightenment failed to satisfy the soul. The scientific method is useful, but it is limited. Consumerism fails to satisfy the dependent culture. Our society is drowning in its own foolishness. The restoration of society must begin with the church. The syndicated columnist, Charley Reese, has said, "Religious beliefs have political and social consequences."

If Christians expect to see an improvement in civil, cultural and moral standards, then they must first seek reformation in the church. Today the culture dictates to the church. If we ever expect to see any reformation in the culture, it must begin in the church.

Although Christians are the proper agents of reformation, there is a sense in which they must understand that reformation is God's own work. For an indeterminate period of time, man has tried to reform himself. However, it's like putting a band aid on cancer. Mans efforts are temporary at best and finally will not stand the test.

The inspired apostle said, "we speak wisdom among those who are mature, yet not the wisdom of this age, nor the rulers of this age, who are coming to nothing" (1 Corinthians 2:6).

So, what are Christians supposed to do? First they must understand the biblical concept called reformation. It is the discovery or re-discovery of biblical truth. Then they have to understand the realities of reformation. We know that wicked men will not seek reformation. Wicked men do not realize there is a future punishment for them. The wicked unreformed men of Sodom could not see the wrath and punishment of God that was about to befall them.

Another reason wicked men will not seek reformation is that they have no thought of eternity. Therefore, they suppress the fear of God's wrath and eternal punishment by trying to

9. Natural Man

focus their attention on something else. In the modern world consumerism became a way to find temporary relief.

Unfortunately, many professing Christians have little or no concern about the future of the church, so reformation is unimportant. Others have a vital interest in the future of the church and for them reformation is an absolute necessity.

God's people know that they must be constantly reformed by the Word of God. They also know it is no small task. It appears that the world is against being reformed by the Word of God. So it is and that is for one simple reason, natural man cannot be reformed.

Spiritual wisdom is necessary for reformation. However, Paul speaks of "God's wisdom in a mystery" (1 Corinthians 2:7). A Biblical mystery is not Gnosticism. Gnosticism was "a religious movement that stressed salvation through knowledge. They were concerned as to how to obtain knowledge" (*Theological Terms in Layman Language*, by Martin Murphy, p. 58).

The mystery Paul mentioned in his letter to the Corinthians can be nothing else than divine secrets that God may choose to reveal at His pleasure. The mystery becomes known to God's people as it pleases God to illumine their minds and change their wills. For the elect in Jesus Christ those divine secrets, as they are revealed, become sensible for their own good and God's glory.

The doctrine of God's eternal decree is relative to the mystery of spiritual wisdom (1 Corinthians 2:7). God predetermined that some people would know and understand the things of the Spirit of God and others would not know and understand the things of the Spirit of God. "But the natural man does not receive the things of the Spirit of God, for they are foolishness to him; nor can he know them, because they are spiritually discerned" (1 Corinthians 2:14).

It is very plain from this text that natural man does not have a spiritual understanding of divine things. God's ordaining hand does not give natural man the ability to receive the things of the Spirit of God.

The terminology "natural man" does not refer to man as God naturally created him, but natural in his fallen human estate. In other words the unregenerate man or woman is in mind when the inspired apostle refers to the natural man. Natural man and the wisdom of God are in stark contrast to each other. There are two categories of wisdom found in Paul's letter to the Corinthian Church. However, Christians must be very careful to distinguish between the two.

1. The wisdom of the world or as Paul prefers to call it human wisdom.

2. The wisdom of God is wisdom known by Christians who know the mind of Christ which is found in the Word of God by the power of the Holy Spirit.

Wisdom necessitates knowledge, so how do we distinguish between natural knowledge and spiritual knowledge? Do unregenerate men have some knowledge of God? The apostle Paul says that ungodly and unrighteous men suppress the truth in unrighteousness, because what may be known of God is manifest in them, for God has shown it to them. "For since the creation of the world His invisible attributes are clearly seen, being understood by the thing that are made, even His eternal power and divine nature, so that they are without excuse, because although they knew God, they did not glorify Him as God, nor were thankful, but became futile in their thoughts and their foolish hearts were darkened" (Romans 1:20-21). The darkened heart is void of spiritual knowledge. If there is no spiritual knowledge, there is no reformation.

There are very religious men who speak about the nature and character of God, the Trinity, Christ, and how sin

9. Natural Man

has affected the human race. Such a man might even talk about principles of religion in such a way that he may seem to be a devout believer. They may attend worship or other activities with the church and give the outward appearance that the Christian religion influences their lives. The inspired apostle Paul warned the church that false religion would invade the church, even if it appears to be true religion. "Therefore take heed to yourselves and to all the flock, among which the Holy Spirit has made you overseers, to shepherd the church of God which He purchased with His own blood. For I know this, that after my departure savage wolves will come in among you, not sparing the flock, Also from among yourselves men will rise up, speaking perverse things to draw away the disciple after themselves" (Acts 20:28ff).

Hypocrisy will ever plague the church with religious men seeking all kinds of knowledge. However for the natural man this natural knowledge is devoid of the knowledge of the excellencies of the divine nature of God.

The natural man may hear about divine excellencies and natural man may even say they are excellent. Natural man may be able to make speeches about the holiness and majesty of God, but natural man cannot attest to the reality of his profession.

The gospel message is meaningless to natural and wicked men who are unreformed. For instance, what good is the resurrection if it is not true? We know that unreformed natural and wicked men do not believe the resurrection is true?

The Word of God makes it clear that "natural man does not receive the things of the Spirit of God." Since natural man does not have an experimental knowledge of the saving work of God, natural man only speculates about the excellencies of God. Natural man sees the saving work of God as foolishness or stupidity, because natural man cannot discern the saving work of God or the beauty of the excellences of God. On the other hand the regenerate man, the true child of God, receives the things of the Spirit of God.

There is a big difference in spiritual knowledge and the knowledge expressed by natural man.

1. Spiritual knowledge transforms the heart. This is substantial, inward, compelling and affective. Even though natural man has knowledge of God and the things of God, it simply has no affect on him.

2. Spiritual knowledge purifies the soul, but the knowledge of natural man leaves the soul in a confused state.

3. Spiritual knowledge gives comfort to the soul because it is the product of truth. Truth is equal to reality, so spiritual knowledge is a testimony of that which is really real.

Dr. Gordon Clarke made a rather astute observation that is worth mentioning. Clarke said, "sensual man (natural man) does not welcome truth as a guest in his home. That is, he does not accept divine truths as true. He does not believe them. This does not mean that he does not understand them." There are plenty of people who have some understanding of God's saving grace, but they reject it and prefer their own way of salvation.

I understand that God is sovereign, but I often wonder why God does not give us a sudden powerful reformation in the church. I work for reformation and pray for reformation, but God has been pleased to withhold any serious reformation in the contemporary church. Even though natural man cannot be reformed it is the duty of all Christians to seek reformation and pray that God will change the heart of natural man. The responsibility for reformation devolves upon God's children, because they have been given the Spirit of God.

9. Natural Man

As the apostle Paul said, "we speak wisdom among those who are mature." It is those who are mature in Christ that will be the agents of reformation.

I urge to you put aside the changeable, presumptuous and fallible wisdom of this world and seek that divine, eternal, and perfect wisdom from above. Then God may be pleased to give us reformation.

10. Sin Is...

As it is written: "There is none righteous, no, not one; There is none who understands; There is none who seeks after God. They have all turned aside; They have together become unprofitable; There is none who does good, no, not one. Their throat is an open tomb; With their tongues they have practiced deceit; The poison of asps is under their lips; Whose mouth is full of cursing and bitterness. Their feet are swift to shed blood; Destruction and misery are in their ways; And the way of peace they have not known. There is no fear of God before their eyes." Now we know that whatever the law says, it says to those who are under the law, that every mouth may be stopped, and all the world may become guilty before God. Therefore by the deeds of the law no flesh will be justified in His sight, for by the law is the knowledge of sin.
Romans 3:10-20

"As the deer pants for the water brooks, so my soul pants for Thee, O God" (Psalm 42:1). Why does the soul thirst for God? Although there are several answers to that question, the soul of man has the inclination to worship. Those without the spirit of God create idols to worship. Those with the spirit of God worship Him in spirit and truth. With or without the spirit of God, every human being craves to worship something. Having lived among the human race for the past sixty five years, I conclude that all of us humans worship "self" to a greater or lesser degree. We either try to look good or feel good. If we fail we try to invent a god that will make us look good or feel good. If good is a non-moral concept then everyone is relatively good. However if good is used in the moral sense, then God alone is good (Mark 10:17).

Over the past twenty years, I have devoted considerable time and effort researching the church growth movement in the evangelical church. This research project revealed the effect of modernity in the life of the church. The inquiry left me in a desert of despair. The influence of culture on the church caused me to feel empty in the face of reality. My feeling was like being in a desert without any water. I wanted to see the church without the ungodly cultural influences. Then with hope in my heart sometimes I thought I could see God working to restore the church. In most cases my hope was dashed, because it was just a mirage. Jesus used rather harsh language, but I'll let Him describe ungodly cultural influences. "Woe to you, scribes and Pharisees, hypocrites! For you are like whitewashed tombs which indeed appear beautiful outwardly, but inside are full of dead men's bones and all uncleanness. Even so you also outwardly appear righteous to men, but inside you are full of hypocrisy and lawlessness" (Matthew 23:27-28). The thirst for an intimate relationship with the Lord is not merely a feeling; it is real. Are you thirsting after God? Are you looking for a cool stream in the desert of despair? Go to God because He alone is good and He is able to satisfy your thirst.

"I've been saved, sanctified, and satisfied" is a tongue and cheek aphorism used to describe a professing Christian who has no thirst for God. I am thankful that salvation is a gift from God and that sanctification is a work of God's grace in my life, but I never achieved satisfaction. There have been times in my Christian experience when I wanted to believe that my soul was satisfied, but I knew better. The church growth movement did not satisfy my soul. I investigated the emotional fervor of the charismatic movement, the higher life of the Keswick movement, and the legalistic pietism so often practiced among alleged conservative churches. I attempted to satisfy my soul by doing something rather than seeking the true and living God. Through the hills and valleys and by the grace of God, my thirsty soul found satisfaction in the truth and

10. Sin Is...

perfection of God. The soul that feels empty and deserted must drink from the pool of God's peace and grace.

One of the least discussed biblical doctrines of our time is total depravity. We simply ignore the doctrine that teaches human beings are born in sin. The Bible clearly states, the doctrine by the inspired Psalmist. "Behold, I was brought forth in iniquity, and in sin my mother conceived me" (Psalm 51:5). Total depravity explains how sin affects the soul (mind, emotions, will) and body. God is sinless and hates sin. The outcome is war. Yes, man and God are at war and the only solution is a peace treaty. The peace treaty goes into effect when God grants new life, new spiritual life, to the soul of man. As the apostle Paul says, "We have peace with God" (Romans 5:1). Jonathan Edwards believed, "peace with God is that state of a believer whereby he is in reconciliation and favor with his Creator."

When we face days, weeks, months, or years of thirst for peace, we must remember as Calvin did that "peace is a free gift and flows from the pure mercy of God." God's peace is the most comforting peace we can experience. His peace was foreordained before the foundation of the world; it is everlasting, and most important our peace was purchased with the blood of Jesus Christ, the prince of peace. God's peace is not only comforting; it is effectual to relieve fear and uncertainty. "Peace I leave with you; my peace I give to you; not as the world gives, do I give to you. Let not your heart be troubled, nor let it be fearful" (John 14:27). Drink deeply from the cool refreshing stream of God's peace.

Years ago a visit to the local grocery store would find the butcher cheerfully greeting me by asking, "How do you feel this morning." I replied by saying, "I feel good." Sometimes I didn't feel good, but I said it. Back then I didn't even know the meaning of good. One day I felt good, but the next day I might feel bad and the next day I feel indifferent. Our feelings may change, but God's peace will never change. I learned from Scripture that no one is good, except God. Now that I have a better understanding of the truth and goodness of God, the integrity of God floods my soul with the hope and assurance of God's peace. I cling to God's integrity during those dry spells in my life. It is those true and reliable words from God that sustains me in the desert of despair. Your feelings and emotions will let you down, but God's truth will fill your soul with heaven's eternal spring of truth.

The thirsty souls of Christians may receive some satisfaction intuitively and emotionally, but they may still feel like they are in a vacuum. The people of God should express God's peace and truth in their relationship with other Christians. Relationships are essential for Christian growth. God said in the beginning "it was not good for the man to be alone" (alone = separated). The most intimate and meaningful human relationship is between the husband and wife. Then Christians must expand the scope of their relationships so that they may serve one another in the body of Christ. During some of the most paralyzing droughts in my Christian life, some dear saint came to my aid; maybe with just a kind word or an expression of love and encouragement.

The desert of despair is a very dry place. When we are caught in the desert, we may encounter a mirage occasionally, but false feelings and hopes will never satisfy the soul. Look and drink from the pool that is filled with God's peace and His truth. However, you will never experience God's peace and truth until you first confess that sin is.

The most popular icons associated with Christianity in North America make public statements like "I teach theology without using theological terms." Another is "I preach theology without people knowing it." How is it possible to teach or preach theology, a study of God, without using words that convey a proper view of God and His creation? With all my education and study, I find no answer to that question. Some-

10. Sin Is...

times technical words or phrases are necessary to explain biblical concepts.

The biblical doctrine of sin may not be easy to digest, but without an understanding of sin, one cannot understand the doctrine of God. Sin is the lack of absolute righteousness and perfection of all God's commandments. Any serious study of the Bible will reveal that God has given hundreds of commandments, both moral and reasonable. Evidence and common sense reveals that no man or woman can completely and perfectly keep those commandments.

Total depravity is a concept that explains the biblical doctrine of sin. The word depravity refers to corruption, so sin refers to the total corruption of man, both body and soul. Total depravity is an appropriate concept because it brings the totality of human nature into the picture. It raises the question: Is human nature good or evil? Do people sin because they are sinners by nature or do they sin because of their social and environmental circumstances?

Sin is a technical word and original sin brings more technicalities to our discussion. Let's look at the words. Original refers to the origin of something or that which is first in order. Original sin is a biblical doctrine that refers to the place and the effect of the sin of our first parents, Adam and Eve. The place of original sin is in the total human being, both body and soul. The effect of original sin is the actual sins committed by every human being.

The guilt of Adam's sin, not his sin, is the natural state of man after the Fall. Guilt implies punishment. The inescapable fact for sinful humanity is that God must be pressed out of the mind. The knowledge of God in the mind of men is the haunting punishment for the sin of idolatry. Sinful human beings cannot think about the nature and character of God because they are reminded of the due punishment that will come from God's hand. The way human beings cope with the due punishment is by diversions. Diversions are simply distractions. These diversions are the only relief available for the totally depraved mind. The godless state of mind is always in a state of stupor, confusion, and ever contradicting itself.

Sin relative to the human body is a subject for another time. Sin relative to the soul is the subject before us. The soul consists of the mind, the will and emotions, sometimes referred to as affections. The soul is metaphysical.

The mind encompasses reason, intelligence and all rational thought. Theologians sometimes use the terminology *noetic effect* of original sin to describe a depraved mind. The word *noetic* comes from the Greek word *nous* which is translated "mind" in the New Testament. Adam had a mind (nous, See Romans 1:28), but sin disabled the mind. The intellect and rational processes were corrupt and faulty. The depraved mind has no place for the knowledge of God. A mind without the knowledge of God is a godless mind. Confusion and contradiction become a way of life. A godless mind will result in dysfunctional families and anti-intellectualism. Private judgment becomes the standard for the culture. Cultural elites (the voices of society) capitalize on godless minds, by promoting confusion and contradiction. Post modernity is the cultural result of a godless mind. It takes a supernatural work of the Holy Spirit to renew the mind.

The will is the decision making aspect of the soul. It decides or chooses according to its inclination. Sin caused the will to be inclined to evil. The sinful will cannot choose good, except for selfish purposes. Thus even if it chooses to do good, it is a sinful decision. To put it another way, the motive for doing good is ego driven, not the desire to please God and all His perfections. A few years ago I obtained a copy of handwritten manuscript by Rev. William Graham. It was a series on human nature written in 1796. In it he said, "the appetite and desires embrace all the objects in nature and each suggests its particular object and craves for indulgence, and although some of them subside, others do not and whilst either of these is an action, we are not without desire and consequently not without a motive to solicit our choice." The end is self-deification. That is another technical word which means humans elevate themselves to the place of God.

Another faculty of the soul is the emotions or sometimes called the affections. It expresses the corrupt mind and will. Some of these expressions fall into categories like hate, love, fear, arrogance, joy, sadness and so forth. The depraved mind conceives that some person has hurt him or her, the will decides to get even, and the emotions demonstrate hate rather than forgiveness.

The answer to this problem of sin is not the eradication of sin. The answer is for the sinner to admit that he or she is a sinner. The answer is a change of the soul (mind, will, and emotions). The mind must be renewed, not perfected. The will must be changed to desire good rather than evil. The emotions must take on a new face. The answer is to seek the Lord while He may be found. The answer is to hear the truth of God's saving grace. The answer is to pray that God may change the soul. The answer is to believe on the Lord Jesus Christ.

If you believe in the doctrine of total depravity, you are a likely candidate to believe that Jesus Christ died for your sin nature and the actual sins you commit.

11. Man-Made Religion

And as He spoke, a certain Pharisee asked Him to dine with him. So He went in and sat down to eat. When the Pharisee saw it, he marveled that He had not first washed before dinner. Then the Lord said to him, "Now you Pharisees make the outside of the cup and dish clean, but your inward part is full of greed and wickedness. Foolish ones! Did not He who made the outside make the inside also? But rather give alms of such things as you have; then indeed all things are clean to you. "But woe to you Pharisees! For you tithe mint and rue and all manner of herbs, and pass by justice and the love of God. These you ought to have done, without leaving the others undone. Woe to you Pharisees! For you love the best seats in the synagogues and greetings in the marketplaces. Woe to you, scribes and Pharisees, hypocrites! For you are like graves which are not seen, and the men who walk over them are not aware of them." Then one of the lawyers answered and said to Him, "Teacher, by saying these things You reproach us also." And He said, "Woe to you also, lawyers! For you load men with burdens hard to bear, and you yourselves do not touch the burdens with one of your fingers. Woe to you! For you build the tombs of the prophets, and your fathers killed them. In fact, you bear witness that you approve the deeds of your fathers; for they indeed killed them, and you build their tombs. Therefore the wisdom of God also said, 'I will send them prophets and apostles, and some of them they will kill and persecute,' that the blood of all the prophets which was shed from the foundation of the world may be required of this generation, from the blood of Abel to the blood of Zechariah who perished between the altar and the temple. Yes, I say to you, it shall be required of this generation. "Woe to you lawyers! For you have taken away the key of knowledge. You did not enter in yourselves, and those who were entering in you hindered." And as He said these things to them, the scribes and the Pharisees began to assail Him vehemently, and to cross-examine Him about many things, lying in wait for Him, and seeking to catch Him in something He might say, that they might accuse Him.

Luke 11:37-54

Jesus was quick to seize every opportunity to teach the eternal truth of God's glory and man's salvation. In spite of the strained relationship the Pharisees had with Jesus, they still wanted to talk to Jesus and question Him. Obviously, they were trying to find a flaw in his doctrine that would stand as a formal complaint to the Sanhedrin, the high court of the Jews.

A religious leader invited Jesus to have lunch with him and the religious leader was astonished that Jesus did not wash His hands before eating the meal. The washing was for ceremonial cleansing. Jewish law made this rule, ceremonial washing, in case Jesus had touched a Gentile or in any way ceremonially defiled himself according to rules laid down by prominent Jewish teachers of former days. We call it tradition. Many churches carry on tradition of past years without inquiry into the truthfulness of the interpretation.

When Jesus noted the response of the religious leader, Jesus set out to preach a sermon on the dangers of man-made religion. I'm using the term man-made religion to refer to religious practices that result from man's ideas rather than God's Word. For example, church leaders are quick to say, "We've always done it that way." The real test is this: Is it biblical?

Jesus spoke to the Pharisees, religious leaders, and their law experts present for this luncheon with six woes. The word "woe" in that context probably was a prophetic announcement reminding them of their misery and warning the religious leaders of their evil proclivities. It was also an expression of regret and compassionate grief for these upstanding religious

11. Man-Made Religion

leaders. These biblical woes convert into dangers, more specifically dangers of man-made religion

Man-made religion distorts the Word of God. Jesus said, "For you tithe mint and rue and all manner of herbs." The Pharisees called themselves following the Law of Moses. "All the tithe of the land, whether of the seed of the land or of the fruit of the tree is the Lord's" (Leviticus 27:30). However, these religious leaders had distorted the Word of God. According to the Mishnah, the interpretation of the Jewish law, the herb "rue" was exempt from the tithe.

The Word of God can be distorted either by misrepresentation of misinterpretation. The Pharisees did not understand the Word of God and they were not explaining it correctly. Why did those religious leaders fail to understand? Maybe they were unable to understand the Word of God. Jesus was talking to the Pharisees on another occasion and said to them, "You are not able to listen to my word, because you are of your father the Devil." According to Jesus the religious leaders were operating out of there own unregenerate desires. It is called man-made religion.

A classical example of man-made religion is found in the sermon of the Mount. Jesus said, "You have heard that it was said to those of old, 'You shall not murder, and whoever murders will be in danger of the judgment.' But I say to you that whoever is angry with his brother without a cause shall be in danger of the judgment" (Matthew 5:21-22).

It is easy to distort Scripture through misrepresentation and misinterpretation. God means everything he says, but sometimes God speaks literally and other times he speaks figuratively. For instance a literal statement is, "I am the God of your father, the God of Abraham, Isaac, and Jacob" (Exodus 3:6). "The number of the children of Israel shall be as the sand of the sea" (Hosea 1:10) is a figurative statement. Then God will often explain a figure of speech in another part of the Bible. The Word of God is not difficult; it just requires effort to understand. Nor is it so mysterious that it cannot be understood.

Man-made religion will certainly include man-made worship. We live in an age when secular entertaining psychobabble replaces sacred worship. Today the focus is on the worshipper rather than the object of worship. Professing Christian worshippers seem more interested in entertainment for themselves rather than worshipping the Creator. Who would deny that people worship the things they love and adore with a passion? People love to worship man-made things. John Calvin in his brief monograph *Of Reforming the Church* said "We must hold that first the spiritual worship of God does not consist in external ceremonies, or any other kind of works whatsoever; and that no worship is legitimate unless it be so framed as to have for its only rule the will of him to whom it is performed. Men allow themselves to devise contrary to his command, he not only repudiates as void, but distinctly condemns." From seminary professors to preachers, we are told that worship services must accommodate and make unbelievers comfortable. They are wrong! Worship must be according to God's Word. God's inspired Word is the only possible source to know what God expects in worship.

Man-made religion not only distorts the Word of God it disobeys the Word of God. Jesus said, "You pass by justice and the love of God." If you neglect justice and the love of God, then you are disobedient to the Word of God. "He has told you, O man, what is good; And what does the LORD require of you but to do justice, to love kindness, and to walk humbly with your God (Micah 6:8, *New American Standard Bible*)?

The Pharisees distorted the Word of God by their worthless man-made regulations, but to make matters worse they did not do what God had clearly instructed them to do. The word "justice" is derived from the Greek word *krisis*, which is also translated into English as decision, discernment

11. Man-Made Religion

or judgment. Justice literally means you get what you deserve. Jesus used the word justice in the context of religious leaders who interpreted the law by their own man-made standards. Their own system of justice was their way of salvation. The religious leaders forgot the truth in Scripture to love kindness. In a word, the religious leaders were self-righteous. In his book, *Three Free Sins*, Steve Brown explained the result of self-righteousness. He said, "More important than anything else, self-righteousness will kill any hope we have of ever being free, forgiven, and able to live in some kind of reasonable peace with ourselves." Self-righteousness is the highest form of greed. The wickedness of greed, such as that of the Pharisees, will lead to injustice and anarchy.

Instead of greed, they were instructed to give alms. To give alms is to show compassion to those in need and give gifts according to God's gift. Unfortunately then as today, the church is busy making regulations that are contrary to the Word of God. The result is that the tradition is passed on from one generation to the next and finally disobedience to the Word of God becomes the norm rather than the exception.

Man-made religion is like a thief, it will steal the truth about the law and grace of God. Jesus said, "You have taken away the key of knowledge." What did Jesus mean when he said that the religious experts had taken away the key to knowledge? In the Old Testament just before God allowed the destruction of the Northern Kingdom, he sent a prophet to preach to those who had distorted and disobeyed the Word of God. The prophet Hosea went to the people as God's mouthpiece and said, "My people are destroyed for a lack of knowledge, because you have rejected knowledge" (Hosea 4:6). The Old Testament preachers had not been teaching the truth relative to sin and grace. In the end, God removed the preachers from their post because they had rejected the knowledge of God.

In the gospel of Matthew Jesus explained the result of the Pharisees taking away the key of knowledge. Jesus said, "You shut up the kingdom of heaven against men" (Matthew 23:13). The Pharisees destroyed the doctrine of true religion, a religion that called all men to repent and believe.

The religious leaders known by the term "Pharisees" were the guardians of the Word of God, but they had so distorted and disobeyed the Word of God until finally they stole the Word of God from the ears of the people they taught.

There are religious leaders today who are thieves every time they teach their man-made religion. It may come in the form of theological liberalism. They will try to tell you that the Bible is not really inerrant and infallible. Man-made religion may come in the form of Moralism. They will try to tell you that you must keep the law to be in a favorable relationship with God. Man-made religion is simply that, it is made by man. Teachers of man-made religion will teach wrong doctrine, such as faith precedes regeneration. If that is true then man literally saves himself. Legalism is a term often used to describe man-made religion. Legalist simply strain out the gnat and swallow a camel. For instance, a church may require someone to attend a class that acclimates the person seeking membership in the church to the rules of the church. To require a person to attend a membership class to join a church is unbiblical. The Christian religion will never be completely pure from every stain, but if there is any purity at all, it will be the result of our understanding the Word of God.

The Old Testament church suffered often because the Word of God was not their standard for faith and worship. (See and read 2 Chronicles, chapter 33 and 34). During the reign of Manesseh and his son Amon, there was plenty of error, superstition, and impure religion. Why? Because, they didn't have the Word of God. The enthronement of Josiah as king of Judah brought a sudden and dramatic change to the church of his day. In the 18th year of Josiah's reign, he ordered Shaphan

11. Man-Made Religion

the scribe, Maaseiah the governor, and Joah the recorder to repair the house of the Lord. When these men consulted Hilkiah the high priest, he reported that he had found the Book of the Law of the Lord given by Moses. To use contemporary language, "he found the Bible."

The discovery of the Book of the Law is surrounded with curiosity. The curiosity is found in 2 Chronicles chapter 34 verses 14 - 18.

> Now when they brought out the money that was brought into the house of the LORD, Hilkiah the priest found the Book of the Law of the LORD given by Moses. Then Hilkiah answered and said to Shaphan the scribe, 'I have found the Book of the Law in the house of the LORD.' And Hilkiah gave the book to Shaphan. So Shaphan carried the book to the king, bringing the king word, saying, 'All that was committed to your servants they are doing. And they have gathered the money that was found in the house of the LORD, and have delivered it into the hand of the overseers and the workmen.' Then Shaphan the scribe told the king, saying, 'Hilkiah the priest has given me a book.' And Shaphan read it before the king. (2 Chronicles 34:14-18)

Shaphan was a scribe. The word "scribe" refers to the practice of writing. The scribe would record information as the priest might request in relation to temple worship. The scribe would make written copies of the law. The scribe may write legal documents for the king or any other work that required writing skills. Hilkiah was a priest. The priest, according to the Word of God (Deuteronomy 33:10) was to teach Israel the law of God and lead the people in temple worship. Now I ask you, who should have read the book of the law when it was discovered? Hilkiah the priest, of course, but he didn't. Why?

The answer is in the text that follows. "Thus it happened, when the king heard the words of the Law, that he tore his clothes. Then the king commanded Hilkiah, Ahikam the son of Shaphan, Abdon the son of Micah, Shaphan the scribe, and Asaiah a servant of the king, saying, 'Go, inquire of the LORD for me, and for those who are left in Israel and Judah, concerning the words of the book that is found; for great is the wrath of the LORD that is poured out on us, because our fathers have not kept the word of the LORD, to do according to all that is written in this book.' So Hilkiah and those the king had appointed went to Huldah the prophetess, the wife of Shallum the son of Tokhath, the son of Hasrah, keeper of the wardrobe. (She dwelt in Jerusalem in the Second Quarter.) And they spoke to her to that effect. Then she answered them, "Thus says the LORD God of Israel... (2Chronicles 34:19-22).

The king instructed five men (men mind you) to get a word from the Lord, but where did those men go? They went to a prophetess, rather than following the directions for discovering God's will that were given in the Word of God. The Urim and Thummim were to be used for discovering God's will. (See Exodus 28:30; Numbers 27:21; 1 Samuel. 28:6; and Ezra 2:63).There is some uncertainty about the nature of the objects, but one thing for certain; they were to be worn by the priests, who were men, not women. Urim and Thummim were to be used to obtain God's judgment on a matter.

Acting contrary to the Word of God, what did Shaphan and Hilkiah do? These men did what they had been doing their entire lifetime, they leaned on their own understanding instead of obeying Scripture. They followed the inclinations of man-made religion.

Someone may think that this portion of God's Word is irrelevant because it does not speak to the modern church. But I say it is very relevant. Someone may think Bibles are in great abundance. In fact, there is a great abundance of Bibles that

11. Man-Made Religion

are translated to fit the needs of every man-made religious organization.

Unfortunately, we are in danger of losing the Bible, but not as a volume of literature. Let me put it another way; we are in danger of losing the Word of God.

1. It is possible to lose the word of God because of indifference.

2. It is possible to lose the word of God because the Scriptures are not studied.
3. If the preaching of the word of God is despised, then the Word of God may be lost.
4. It is possible to lose the Word of God because it is considered irrelevant.

Whether we lose the Word of God through neglect, disbelief, or disobedience, we are brought to the same end. There is a question that every Christian ought to ask, privately and individually. The church ought to ask it publicly and collectively. What can I (we) do to maintain the integrity of the Word of God in my life or our lives? The answer I come up with is "make a diligent effort to remove any man-made religion that is set up in my soul." It is not really that difficult, but it will require the abandonment of man-made religion and the adoption of God-made religion.

12. Doctrinal Integrity

For I have not shunned to declare to you the whole counsel of God. Therefore take heed to yourselves and to all the flock, among which the Holy Spirit has made you overseers, to shepherd the church of God which He purchased with His own blood. For I know this, that after my departure savage wolves will come in among you, not sparing the flock. Also from among yourselves men will rise up, speaking perverse things, to draw away the disciples after themselves.
Acts 20:27-30

I believe in God! I believe in Jesus Christ! I believe the Bible teaches predestination. All these are familiar assertions frequently heard from the lips of Christians everywhere. Muslims and Christians believe in God, but which God. The Church of Jesus Christ of Latter-day Saints (the Mormon Church) and the Methodist Church believe in Jesus Christ, but which Jesus Christ. Baptists and Presbyterians believe in predestination, but which view of predestination.

Theological liberals have accused theological conservatives with divisiveness because of doctrine. In fact the war cry of the liberals during the middle of the 20th century was "doctrine divides, service unites." They are wrong. However, I grant that the spirit of the postmodern age opens the door for a form of neo-ecumenism. Doctrine no longer divides because the legitimacy and credibility of a creed has become personal relative among many creedal and confessional churches. (Denial will not ease the pain of the present truth). Every branch of the church has been touched by the postmodern concept, to a greater or lesser degree.

What kind of church and confession are we passing on to the next generation? If churches follow their current neo-ecumenical course, there will be no doctrinal distinctions.

Everyone will do what is right in his own eyes and loudly proclaim that we must agree to disagree. It is not possible to agree to disagree. It is possible to say that one or the other is wrong and maybe both are wrong. To agree to disagree is to fan the fire of ecumenism. It will destroy the church by sophistic deception. We should all remember that Jesus called some churches "synagogues of Satan" because they had a false profession (Revelation 3:9). The only protection the church has from "false professions" is the biblical form of church government. God designed the government of the church to protect it from false doctrine.

The reason that various denominations have so many different gospels and so many different doctrines is that although they may have one common creed, they have an unbiblical form of church government. Churches everywhere seem to have forgotten that God is the governor of the Universe. The Word of God in the Book of Psalms says, "The Lord has established His throne in heaven, and His kingdom rules over all" (Psalm 103:19). God's government must be the factor that determines church government. Common law and humanly devised statute law is not sufficient to rule God's kingdom.

This generation of God's people is past due on their responsibility to call the entire church to task on the very issue that has divided the church. What has divided the church? Is it the doctrine of God's saving grace? Is it the doctrine of God's holiness and man's responsibility? Is it over the consummation of all things? No, the church is divided over the government of His church.

Since we believe the gospel and we believe that born again sinners want to hear the gospel, then it would seem normal and sensible for God to give us the means to preach and teach the gospel and for that matter preach and teach the whole counsel of God. However, the condition necessary for the church to determine who has the right and authority to decide

12. Doctrinal Integrity

which gospel is the right gospel and which doctrine is the right doctrine is biblical church government.

The reason the church is divided and the reason there are so many denominations is they have not determined who has the right and who has the authority to settle a controversy in the church. Paul faced the same dilemma in his day as we face today. There were two different versions of the gospel. In Acts 15 "some men came down from Judea and began teaching the brethren, unless you are circumcised according to the custom of Moses, you cannot be saved. And when Paul and Barnabas had great dissension and debate with them, the brethren determined that Paul and Barnabas and certain others of them should go up to Jerusalem to the apostles and elders concerning this issue" (Acts 15:1, 2). According to one gospel, salvation is by grace through faith in Christ. The other gospel taught salvation by grace through faith in Christ plus the necessity of circumcision according to the custom of Moses. Please notice that Luke brings to our attention the fact that the brethren were the subjects placed under the duplicity of doctrine.

If they are brethren, they should have every desire to settle the controversy. A brother implies kinship, a covenant relationship and therefore a unity of doctrine should be the norm. Instead the church was divided over the question of keeping the law of God for the salvation of the soul. Brethren are sinners and subject to disagree and find themselves on the opposite end of some doctrine, but the Bible makes it clear that Paul could not live with two different gospels. Neither did Paul seek the advice of two church courts. If they were brethren it would seem that they would be willing to discuss the controversy and come to unanimous decision (See Acts 15).

The Governor of the universe gave two principles so His people could establish the biblical form of church government. The first principle is the Word of truth. This principle is called constitutional government. John Calvin recognized this principle in his *Institutes of the Christian Religion*. Under the heading "Necessity of Church Constitutions" Calvin wrote, "many unlettered persons, when they are told that men's consciences are impiously bound by human traditions, and God is worshipped in vain, apply the same erasure to all the laws by which the order of the church is shaped" (*Institutes of the Christian Religion*, 4.10.27). He is right because man-centered worship tends to replace God-centered worship. The same principle applies to the government of the church. Calvin continues, "Yet since such diversity exists in the customs of men, such variety in their minds, such conflicts in their judgments and dispositions, no organization, is sufficiently strong unless constituted with definite laws...Therefore...when churches are deprived of them, their very sinews disintegrate and they are wholly deformed and scattered" (*Institutes of the Christian Religion*, 4.10.27).

God regulates the manner in which the church must be governed. When the church is deprived of God's regulation and God's constitution of church government, then the church is deprived of God's government. At the present time the evangelical church has not agreed on the doctrine of God's government. The prophet Amos left the New Testament church with a question that is easy to answer. "Can two walk together, unless they are agreed?" (Amos 3:3).

God's government is constitutional. However, the contemporary church has heard little if any about God's plan for constitutional church government. There is a tendency to ignore the principles of God's government as unimportant to the congregation and it is not just a recent omission. As important as sound biblical doctrine may be, and sound doctrine is indisputably important, there must be a governing body to maintain sound doctrine.

The government of the church is under the supreme headship of Jesus Christ. It is well known that there must

12. Doctrinal Integrity

proceed from the headship of Christ a particular form of church government. The government of the church is not merely an optional replacement for modernity's Managerialism. The principles of church government must be founded upon the Word of God. Jonathan Edwards, although a Congregationalist, said to the Scottish Presbyterian minister, Ebenezer Erskine, that "as to the Presbyterian government, I have long been perfectly out of conceit of our unsettled, independent, confused way of church government in this land; and the Presbyterian way has ever appeared to me most agreeable to the word of God, and the reason and nature of things" (*The Works of J. Edwards*, Hickman ed., vol. 1, page cxxi). Edwards like so many more seemed content with what they viewed as an unbiblical form of church government, thus denying the ultimate authority given to the elders by the Lord Jesus Christ. The spiritual government of the church is not merely pragmatic or utilitarian. The government of the church is the source of order and authority for the church to carry out its mission. The church cannot carry out its mission of making disciples without sound biblical God appointed church government. It is well known that the church cannot do its work amid chaos and confusion. Therefore Christ appointed elders to rule over His church. These elders or presbyters rule by an ultimate standard, which is the Word of God. In Calvin's Catechism of the Church of Geneva he asked the question: "Is it of importance, then, that there should be a certain order of government established in churches?" The answer was: "It is: they cannot otherwise be well managed or duly constituted. The method is for elders to be chosen to preside as censors of manners, to guard watchfully against offenses, and exclude from communion all whom they recognize to be unfit for it, and who could not be admitted without profaning the sacrament." What will it take to awaken the sleeping giant? The sweet romance for power and money will chase away any hope of reformation and the restoration of a sound biblical church government.

The testimony of our forefathers in the faith is a great help, but finally the Word of God is the constitution upon which God governs His church. The seed of constitutional government was given to Noah. Under the Mosaic covenant, the particular specifications for God's government became more evident. The development of God's government over the Old Testament church actually precedes the law given to Moses at Sinai. If God had not given His sacred government to His people, the law would have been subject to interpretation by man-made autonomy, rather than God-centered theonomy.

The second principle God gave His people to establish a biblical form of church government is "rule by order." The elders in the Old Testament ruled by order, according to God's law (See Exodus 18). The elders made binding decisions. The fashionable "thou shalt not judge" is not God's plan to settle matters of doctrine and practice. In the Old Testament, judgment was the work of the elders at the gate. In the New Testament, judgment is the work of elders who come together as representatives of the church. The immediate thought and words of any Christian is "what about the sinfulness of all men including the elders." True, but the elders were men who had been set aside according to God's constitution. In the Old Testament, the qualifications for the elders were not merely old age. God's constitution says they must be "able men, such as fear God, men of truth, [and] hating covetousness." In the New Testament, the qualifications are more specific than the general qualifications found in the Old Testament. The elders make vows thus calling them to account for the purpose of judicious adjudication of all matters pertaining to doctrine and practice. Therefore care must be taken in the selection and ordination of elders. If the elders are ungodly, unruly, and ill equipped, then their decisions will be ungodly, unruly, and deficient of God's constitutional government. Ungodly men making ungodly

12. Doctrinal Integrity

decisions do not constitute the biblical form of church government we find in Scripture.

The most prominent example of biblical church government previously referred to is found in Acts chapter fifteen. The decision of the court was in agreement with the Word of God. Since the representatives of the court were under constraint to judge justly, they could not possibly disagree with the Word of God. When a decision is contradictory to the Word of God, then the constitutional principle was abused or ignored. An ungodly decision does not come from a godly church court. Furthermore godly people must not obey an ungodly decision. Thomas Witherow left the church this challenge.

> If our distinctive principles are not apostolic and important…and by standing apart from other denominations upon such a ground, we only perpetuate needless divisions in the Church of God. If we discover that the peculiarities of the system [doctrine of church government] are either not true, or truths of minor consequence, we should take speedy steps to heal the schism that exists, and exemplify Christian union on a large scale by uniting with some sister sect, whose principles are more Scriptural and important than our own. But if on the other hand, our distinctive principles are very important as well as true, then duty to God and the Church demands that we avow, illustrate, and defend them, and press them on the notice of the world. (*The Apostolic Church, Which is It?*, p. 60, by Thomas Witherow)

13. Anger

But You, O Lord, are a God full of compassion, and gracious, Longsuffering [slow to anger] *and abundant in mercy and truth.*

Psalm 86:15

The word anger or angry is a condition of the fallen human race. The soul of man consists of the mind, will, and emotions. The mind understands anger, the will is inclined to anger and the emotions express anger. The word anger is about as hard to define as the word love. My purpose in listing this brief summary of biblical texts is not to purely define the word anger, but rather to show in contradistinction to the popular Christian psychological movement that anger is not merely a communicative expression. I've heard Christians say that anger is expressed by facial contortions or the volume of one's vocal expression or any composure that seems displeasing to the recipient. Then there are those who equate anger with contemptuousness and contentiousness. Contemptuousness refers to an arrogant and defiant person. Contentiousness refers to hostility and strife.

Anger is a biblical concept associated with that dimension of the soul called the affections in previous centuries, but now generally referred to as the emotions. Any expression of the emotions may be sinful or it may be righteous. The only way that sinful men, and all men are sinful, may interpret an emotional concept is to understand the biblical teaching of that particular concept, whether it is love, anger, hate, et al. God's anger is evident from the Word of God.

God becomes angry with His children, Israel in the Old Testament and the church in the New Testament. Sometimes God becomes angry when His people are displeased with His providence. "Now when the people complained, it displeased the LORD; for the LORD heard it, and His anger was aroused. So the fire of the LORD burned among them, and consumed some in the outskirts of the camp" (Numbers 11:1). False worship will provoke God's anger. "When you beget children and grandchildren and have grown old in the land, and act corruptly and make a carved image in the form of anything, and do evil in the sight of the LORD your God to provoke Him to anger..." (Deuteronomy 4:25). A disregard for God's holiness will provoke His anger. "Then the anger of the LORD was aroused against Uzza, and He struck him because he put his hand to the ark; and he died there before God" (1 Chronicles 13:10). God's anger against His disobedient church should cause His church to repent and reform according to His Word. Isaiah chapter five is a text to remember especially the awesome response of God toward His disobedient church of the Old Testament. "Therefore the anger of the LORD is aroused against His people; He has stretched out His hand against them and stricken them, and the hills trembled. Their carcasses were as refuse in the midst of the streets. For all this His anger is not turned away, but His hand is stretched out still" (Isaiah 5:25).

    The Lord Jesus Christ in his humanity is said to have been angry. "And when He had looked around at them with anger, being grieved by the hardness of their hearts, He said to the man, 'Stretch out your hand.' And he stretched it out, and his hand was restored as whole as the other" (Mark 3:5).

    Men of God such as Jacob (Gen. 31:36), Moses (Exodus 16:20), David (2 Samuel 13:21), Nehemiah (Nehemiah 5:6), et. al. are said to be angry. The Bible clearly teaches that there is an anger that is not sinful. In fact, Christians are commanded to be angry without sinning (Ephesians 4:26).

    My purpose is to show that anger is not necessarily, although it may be, sinful, nor can anger be attributed to outward expressions. Very often in Scripture, which is to be

13. Anger

our rule, anger is associated with the intent and practice of punishment. Jay Adams explains the uses of anger.

> The energies of anger are wasted and used damagingly when they are directed solely toward oneself or another. Under control, anger is to be released within oneself and toward others only in ways that motivate one to confront others in a biblical manner in order to solve problems. Anger is a powerful emotion. But its power to motivate must be used, not abused. This motivating power is used properly when it drives one to begin to rectify any wrong situation between brethren as quickly as possible. It is used biblically when it impels one to become reconciled to his brother immediately" [Matthew 5;22] (*The Christian Counselors Manual*, by Jay Adams, p. 354 - 355).

So in the final analysis when someone is charged with sinful anger, it means that angry person intends to inflict pain, harm, and/or damage on a person, rather than deal with the problem that originally caused the anger.

Please look at the following Old Testament passages carefully to see how anger is directed toward an object, which results in pain, suffering, or harm. (The following are taken from the *New American Standard Bible*).

Genesis 49:6 - Let my soul not enter into their council; Let not my glory be united with their assembly; Because in their **anger** they slew men, And in their self-will they lamed oxen.

Exodus 22:24 - My **anger** will be kindled, and I will kill you with the sword; and your wives shall become widows and your children fatherless.

Exodus 32:12 - Why should the Egyptians speak, saying, 'With evil intent He brought them out to kill them in the mountains and to destroy them from the face of the earth'? Turn from Thy burning **anger** and change Thy mind about doing harm to Thy people.

The following words, in bold and underlined, found in the New Testament are translated from the Greek word *thumos*. It is an visible expression of an inward disposition.

2 Corinthians 12:20 - For I am afraid that perhaps when I come I may find you to be not what I wish and may be found by you to be not what you wish; that perhaps there may be strife, jealousy, **angry** tempers, disputes, slanders, gossip, arrogance, disturbances;

Galatians 5:20 - idolatry, sorcery, enmities, strife, jealousy, outbursts of **anger**, disputes, dissensions, factions,

Luke 4:28 - And all in the synagogue were filled with **rage** as they heard these things;

Acts 19:28 - And when they heard this and were filled with **rage**, they began crying out, saying, "Great is Artemis of the Ephesians!"

Revelation 16:19 - And the great city was split into three parts, and the cities of the nations fell. And Babylon the great was remembered before God, to give her the cup of the wine of His **fierce** wrath.

Hebrews 11:27 - By faith he left Egypt, not fearing the **wrath** of the king; for he endured, as seeing Him who is unseen.

Matthew 2:16 - Then when Herod saw that he had been tricked by the magi, he became very **enraged**, and sent and slew all the male children who were in Bethlehem and in all its environs,

13. Anger

from two years old and under, according to the time which he had ascertained from the magi.

Another Greek word that refers to anger is *orge*. It often refers to the inner passion of the soul. It does not necessarily have to be sinful, because God becomes angry, but not sinful anger.

Mark 3:5 - And after looking around at them with **anger**, grieved at their hardness of heart, He said to the man, "Stretch out your hand." And he stretched it out, and his hand was restored.

Revelation 14:10 - he also will drink of the wine of the **wrath** of God, which is mixed in full strength in the cup of His anger; and he will be tormented with fire and brimstone in the presence of the holy angels and in the presence of the Lamb.

Ephesians 4:31 - Let all bitterness and wrath and **anger** and clamor and slander be put away from you, along with all malice.

John 3:36 - He who believes in the Son has eternal life; but he who does not obey the Son shall not see life, but the **wrath** of God abides on him.

Romans 1:18 - For the **wrath** of God is revealed from heaven against all ungodliness and unrighteousness of men, who suppress the truth in unrighteousness.

Ungodly anger is a menace to the good health of the soul and sometimes for the physical body. Individual relationships are destroyed because of anger. Churches are divided because of anger. Wars are started because of anger. Listen carefully to the words of the Lord Jesus Christ. "I say to you that whoever is angry with his brother without a cause shall be in danger of the judgment" (Matthew 5:22). To avoid the danger of judgment, eliminate the anger that festers in your soul, make peace with God (Isaiah 27:5), then make peace with your siblings in the family of God.

14. Marriage

Therefore a man shall leave his father and mother and be joined to his wife, and they shall become one flesh.
Genesis 2:24

This chapter of *The Present Truth* is about the present discombobulation of the marriage institution. Marriage is a divine institution originating within God's covenant with man at creation. To understand this institution properly there are chronological factors that must be applied to the logic of the institution. Man, a male being, was created first. God created man to have dominion by the labor of his hands and the propagation of his own kind. Since man was alone, he had no mutual help to fulfill the covenant responsibilities. God provided the woman, one of man's own kind, for mutual help.

God created a male and female human being that constitute a married couple (See Genesis 1:27). As in everything God does you will find order and harmony. The Lord said, "I will make him a helper comparable to him" (Genesis 2:18). Although there are several renderings of the phrase "helper comparable to him", the essence of the text is that the woman is just right for the man. The woman made man complete.

After this remarkable creation, God brought the woman to man, thus forming the divine institution commonly known as marriage. Marriage is an ordinance of God's creative work. Marriage is not a sacrament and marriage, as an institution, does not belong to God's redemptive plan.

Now we have to ask, what happened to this divine institution? Sin entered the world. Sin does not change the fact that God ordained marriage and therefore God must regulate marriage. In fact, sin is all the more reason that marriage must be God regulated.

A careful examination of the Word of God will reveal the fundamental principles necessary for a biblical marriage and therefore a biblical family.

Marriage is honorable. (Hebrews 13:4)

The woman is necessary for the man. (Gen. 2 and 1 Corinthians 11:11-12)

The man is the head in marriage. (1 Peter 3:1-7; Colossians 3:18; Ephesians 5:22)

The honor and necessity of marriage is rarely questioned by any culture, because in most cultures males and females marry. In most cultures the government of the marriage is closely defined. In America, that is not the case.

Mr. Buck Hatch former professor at Columbia International University explained some of the problems in America for the institution of marriage.

Failure to pick a suitable mate.

Once a mate has been chosen the failure to work out relationship rules that will be durable and equitable.

Democracy is the primary government in marriage, even though it is unbiblical.

The western culture has three kinds of government in the marriage.

- The husband is manager
- The wife is manager
- The husband and wife are co-managers

14. Marriage

Which do you think is the biblical form of management? The model is the holy Trinity - Father, Son, and Holy Spirit. In the Trinity, it is clear from the Bible that God the Father makes the decisions and plans.

When the husband attempts to manage, he often acts like a tyrant. A tyrant exercises authority, headship, and makes decisions; but, what motivates the tyrant? Is it love or justice? The answer is no, no. A tyrant cannot exercise justice because he is motivated by his egocentricity. I expect much of male headship in the home is tyranny. The godly biblical prescription is dismissed as impossible in our permissive society.

The authority of the man in a marriage relationship begins with the primary duty, which the bible describes as love. Sentiment is not love. Sentiment is ones opinion or ones feeling toward someone else. Spontaneous sentiment is not biblical love. In a biblical marriage sentiment diminishes as love increases. What are some of the reasons that men fail to love their wives? First the husband is the representative of love; it falls upon him to love. Then man's egotistic struggle for power overrules the biblical mandate to fulfill the role of the head of the house. The Bible teaches that men are responsible for the care of the family.

All the reasons are distorted by sin. Every government must have a recognized head. Ultimately all authority comes from God. God is the head of all, but in the family this dreaded responsibility to act with authority falls upon the husband.

R. L. Dabney wrote a young recently wed student a few words about marriage. "I regard the rich affections of two young hearts, united by chaste and virtuous aspirations…a sacred and precious thing. Would to God all old people could preserve throughout the tenderness of those affections. They are on loan from God, to be jealously cherished; and to be made mutually as abiding and sweet as this rude world will permit" (*Life and Letters of R. L. Dabney*, p. 247). To jealously cherish the marriage institution is a noble goal in life.

The following covenant is one I suggest for every married couple.

I AM/I WANT

I have the "I am/I want" syndrome because of the remains of the sin nature in me. The "I am/I want" syndrome leads to pride and lusts of all sorts. The "I am/I want" syndrome is a problem in reality and experience. God's immeasurable grace is more than sufficient to overcome my inability and sinfulness as I struggle against the evil forces that would destroy my marriage and family.

I will deal with my own personal life by saturating myself in the Word of God. I will be sensitive to the application of the Word of God to my life.

The strategy to overcome the "I am/I want" syndrome must be accompanied by the Holy Spirit in the life of the Christian. I must recognize that the "I am/I want" syndrome will bug me throughout this life, but I will be fully delivered in the life to come. I consider myself "in progress" toward that goal.

Dated_____

_____
(Husband)

_____

14. Marriage

(Wife)

15. Education

... I will teach you the good and the right way.
1 Samuel 12:23

University education appeared as an institution in the twelfth century. Most universities were under the authority of the Roman Catholic Church. The corruption of the Roman Catholic Church infected the university with a fatal form of secularism. However, the concept of the university brought intellectual and literary life together at a time when the western culture wanted to find unity in diversity. Unfortunately, the university has become the arena for diabolical thought. The root of the fundamental failure of the university system is in its failure to practicalize its educational theory.

The church historian, Phillip Schaff, brings to light how the university was a well-intended dragon. The university recognized "theology" as the queen of the sciences. "Theology was known as the highest and master study. Alexander IV., writing to Paris, 1256, said that theology ruled over the other studies like a mistress, and they followed her as servants (*History of the Christian Church*, Philip Schaff). It was the failure of the Roman Catholic Church to give the university theological truth. A bad systematic theology will produce a bad world and life view. An educational institution is a most religious institution, but religious in the bad sense of the word. The true religion is reserved for God's covenant people. It is time for the university to be absorbed by the academy.

The academy model is not explicitly defined in Scripture, however the Bible is useful to guide any culture with fundamentals that are favorable to the academy model for education. The academy is designed to allow for a mentoring relationship between the teacher and the student. The academy ought to be an extension of the familial instruction. "You shall teach them diligently to your children, and shall talk of them when you sit in your house, when you walk by the way, when you lie down, and when you rise up" (Deuteronomy 6:7). The mentoring process was used to educate the great men in ancient times. To be at the foot of a great teacher is a matter of common sense. Paul said, "I am indeed a Jew, born in Tarsus of Cilicia, but brought up in this city at the feet of Gamaliel, taught according to the strictness of our fathers' law, and was zealous toward God as you all are today" (Acts 22.3). *The New American Standard Bible* uses the terminology "educated under Gamaliel." In his book *"The Passion of the Western Mind"*, Richard Tarnas traces the academy to Plato's model for education.

> Under Plato's guidance, the classical *paideia* assumed the deeper metaphysical and spiritual dimensions of the Academy, an institution as much monastery as university, holding forth the ideal of inner perfection realized through disciplined education. (*The Passion of the Western Mind*, p. 43, by Richard Tarnas)

Any philosophy of education will include a more or less consistent world and life view. A Christian world and life view is a consistent system of disciplines necessary for any education to take place. It is called a Christian education. Democratic idealism, enlightenment thinking, or a natural rights theory must not shape Christian education. Revelation and more specifically "special revelation" must shape Christian education.

Education must be defined for any progress in this discussion. The word "education" is often used to describe the general process of passing information to others. To put it another way, education has become a generic term, concept, and philosophy used by people who have an agenda for passing along, sometimes objective, but primarily subjective ideas.

15. Education

There are two Greek words that are translated educate. *Paideuo*, although translated educate primarily referred to the process of training children. Sometimes the word *paideuo* was translated discipline, which naturally accompanies training. The concept of training a child fits the description of a school or the university. The school is the place where a teacher gives information to a scholar. The scholar learns, *paideuo*, from the teacher. Therefore, it may be said that education is that process whereby a teacher passes along information to a student who may be subject to discipline if the student ignores the instruction. The result would be that the student would have enough information to carry out certain duties in life.

Another Greek word *manthano* is also translated "to educate." The Greek word *manthano* may be traced to another Greek word *math* from which we get the English word "mathematics". Plato used this word to refer to "the mathematical sciences, especially arithmetic, geometry, and astronomy." It was used by Greek philosophers such as Parmenides, 475 B.C., through the New Testament era into the first century. It primarily, but not exclusively, referred to the process of learning by study. It appears that the early Greek thinkers associated the word with rational, logical, and empirical disciplines.

The purpose of education is not to pass on information from one generation to the other. Information must be passed on, but the best way to pass on information is by training. Train your child to speak with a Southern accent, but teach them to use correct grammar. Train your child to memorize multiplication tables, but teach them to use logic in solving mathematical problems. Passing on information has destroyed one generation after the other. Dr. Harold Parker explains how church historians make so many serious errors in reporting church history inaccurately. "The second error lies in the tendency for the student to follow the authority ahead of him in Indian file, deeper and deeper into the morass of error. If the first of the secondary authorities is wrong in fact or judgment, then all who follow him will be in error also, for they are on the same path. They will remain in error until the primary sources are checked again" (*Studies in Southern Presbyterian History*, by Harold Parker, p. 56). Passing erroneous information from one generation to the next is not education. Education must take place in an environment where the student can consult an authority in the learning process. The authority can be no other than *God's* revelation and God's *Revelation*. That which seems right in the eyes of a man may not actually exist in reality.

The spirit of egalitarianism is like the individualism of democracy. It is an enemy to intellectual stimulation. The enlightenment thinker is without a foundation or a purpose. Science, rationality, and empirical or metaphysical inquiry will not establish an infallible intellectual agenda. Naturally, natural rights theorists are disinclined toward a definitive set of rules and regulations from an infallible source.

The recovery of a Christian world and life view applied to the philosophy of education will be the means by which Christian education will thrive. Once recovered the philosophy of education must include ontological and teleological dimensions.

Does education actually exist? Dr. R. L. Dabney said, "education is a soul function" (*The Practical Philosophy*, by R. L. Dabney, p. 341). If education is a "soul function" then it must have its root in the soul. If there is no soul, there can be no education. Dabney has said it so well let him speak. "The modern American State is a political corporation. 'Corporations have no souls.' Can there be a greater solecism than to assign the training of souls to agents which have no souls?" (*The Practical Philosophy,* p. 341). If people who submit their lives to a godless state and allow that state to teach Covenant children, there is no education of the children. Therefore, there is no ontological basis for an educational system.

15. Education

Does education have a final purpose? At this juncture, the meaning of the word "educate" comes into play. If an education serves the purpose of preparing someone to earn a livelihood, then what is the purpose of training? However, the case has already been made that one prepares for his or her life work by training. A person enters an apprenticeship program to learn how to earn a living. The purpose of an education is to prepare the mind for God's call in life. God's call may include familial, civil, and religious aspects. An education prepares for that call.

The reality of the existence of education and the final purpose of education depends upon truth. Methodology, content, sincerity or any other human motive will not insure the education of children or adults. It is dangerous to believe that you can send your children to Sodom for their education and expect them to return to the mountains to live out their *soul* purpose. The education and training of ministers during the early part of the nineteenth century was difficult as it is in any generation. In tracing the history of the Southern Presbyterian Church during that period, we find the Sodom effect on the students. (Lot and his family really liked the big city). The students "who went north to study theology seldom returned" because the comforts, money, and promises of easy ministerial positions were more pleasing to the eye in the big cities than the difficult ministry in the old southwest. The self-perpetuation of the universities in the western world has destroyed the historical and biblical approach to education. The academy model was and still is apropos to this present time. That which is true and real is timeless.

In 1912, Dr. J. Gresham Machen lectured to the faculty and students at Princeton Seminary on "The Scientific Preparation of the Minister." Dr. Machen said, "Our whole system of school and college education is so constituted as to keep religion and culture as far apart as possible and ignore the question of the relationship between them" (*Education,*

Christianity, and the State, by J. Gresham Machen, p. 46). History proves the result of a godless education.

The academy model will recover reality and purpose in education. An academy education will examine metaphysics and physics; the rational with the empirical. An academy education will include the rules for intelligent logical and rational inquiry. The academy will restore the right place for biblical ethics. An academy education will take the educational responsibility away from a godless, self-perpetuating university and return to the covenant parents. The responsibility rests upon the shoulders of parents to educate their children by the authority given in God's Revelation. Dr. R. L. Dabney reminds us of the dangers of a godless state. The State will:

> intentionally pervert her education power to corrupt ends...the family is a circle of social jurisdiction more strongly entitled to exist than the State itself; that the Creator and the light of Nature point out the parents as the proper heads of the family, clothed with a higher and more inviolable authority over their children than any magistrate has over his fellow-citizens; that since it is wrong to do evil that good may come, no professed expediency can justify the usurpation of the parents' prerogative by another and lower power; that such usurpation is an inexpedient and needless as it is unjust, because the best educational results are always obtained where the State recognizes the rights of parents and individuals... (*The Practical Philosophy*, p. 342-343).

The raging culture wars have a long string of wounded soldiers and citizens in this world. The most devastating battle is the attack against the minds of young people. The specific culture war I have in mind is education and more specifically education in the Christian sector.

15. Education

Christians are notorious propagators of false concepts leading to an unbiblical world and life view. One such notorious idea is that covenant children may be farmed out to the church for their education or even to a pagan ungodly government school. Where did Christians find such a silly notion? I don't intend to answer that question, because even if I did, it wouldn't help the sorry condition of elementary, secondary, or higher education.

We have a large volume of books, monographs, and scholarly articles that review the atrocious history of how we got in this mess. What we don't believe or think we have is a solution. The words "believe and think" should apply only to the pagan culture. Christians do have an answer.

Christians should be in the forefront of reforming education in this country, a concept not so new. In Martin Luther's *An Appeal to the Ruling Class of German Nationality as to the Amelioration of the State of Christendom*, Luther argued for reformation of education. Luther said, "the universities need a sound and thorough reformation." Luther's concern was that the Church of Rome was corrupt to the degree that "everything that the papacy has instituted or ordained is directed solely toward the multiplication of sin and error. Unless they are completely altered from what they have been hitherto, the universities will fit exactly what is said in the Book of Maccabees: 'places for the exercise for youth, and for the Greekish fashion'... . Nothing could be more wicked, or serve the devil better, than unreformed universities."

Reformation is necessary, but not like Luther wanted reform. Luther wanted to repair public education. The reformation I have in mind must replace public education and the university model.

The primary reason for the replacement is the bankruptcy of public education at all levels. Modernity and its replacement, the postmodern concept, have significantly constituted the bankruptcy.

The driving force of modernity is progress. The tools that make progress possible are many. However, for the sake of this discussion, pragmatism, relativism, and utilitarianism are the major world views that influence public education.

Modernity is a force to be reckoned with, but the force will eventually fail. It must because it is humanistic and not divine. It is proximate and not ultimate. Human autonomy is self-destructive. Divine aseity is the source of the ultimate authority and supreme power. Aseity refers to "existence originating from and having no source other than itself" (*Webster Dictionary*). If any educational system survives, it does so because it has ultimate authority to fulfill its purpose. Supreme power must accompany that authority or otherwise some other power will win the day.

Modern educators focus on the proximate rather than the ultimate. I don't hear Christians say, "What does God say about education?" I do hear them say, "What does William James say about education?" A few Christians might ask, "what did John Calvin say about education?" We cannot replace or repair our educational institutions and systems by consulting sinful men. Of course, it is wise to consult the church fathers that went before us, but the ultimate authority must be the Word of God.

The postmodern educational philosophy is no help in the restoration of educational philosophy. In fact, postmodern thought is even more reason to replace the present model. The postmodern educators have effectively created the religion of education as a means to change the culture. After the failure of the enlightenment and its progeny, the postmodernists have made educational philosophy a god of the new age.

Herbert Schlossberg accuses the public schools of promoting "the socialization of diverse peoples" and they have been successful in that endeavor. It is sad that Christians, particularly postmodern Christians, have used the educational system in this country to homogenize the variety of cultures

15. Education

that God has set in place. Postmodern educators will not admit that ethnic groups are fundamentally different. To make many cultures into one is not a biblical world and life view.

The philosophical agenda to establish the educational elite has been a miserable failure. One rogue passing along information to other rogues produces a generation of uneducated hypocrites with a diploma to prove they attended a school of higher learning. The travesty is that Christians simply shrug their shoulders.

The educational system proposed by Dewey, Owen, Mann, et al., is a failure by their own standards. Statist education was their goal and all it has produced is an uneducated, uncivilized, and incompetent society that hates its culture of residence.

The academies of colonial America and the academies of the old Southwest were God-centered educational institutions. They resisted the liberal Unitarianism until at last the Unitarians took control of the educational institutions throughout America. The history of those Calvinistic academies shaped the intellectual, cultural, and political lives for many generations. Unfortunately, the godless Unitarian universities have created a tyrannical force that has been the most powerful change agent in this country. Os Guinness believes that the role of American public schools was so successful that they "became almost the working equivalent of a European established church" (*The American Hour*, by Os Guinness, p. 155). He is right because the educational system in America is a rival to Christianity.

The reformation of the educational system in this country will be painful to the socialites, liberals, and statists. However, Christians do not have a choice in the matter. Reforming our educational system is a noble work for God's people.

16. Looking Back

Remember the Law of Moses, My servant, Which I commanded him in Horeb for all Israel, With the statutes and judgments.
                                                        Malachi 4:4

Looking back at the principles derived from Old Testament institutions will benefit the present truth and the present time. The Old Testament is replete with types and symbols found in ceremonial and judicial case law. Types are ordinances that have a prophetic element. Old Testament messianic prophecies had present value, but pointed to future facts. For example, the Passover lamb, and holy of holies represented a type of the work and person of Jesus Christ. Symbols show in visible form a spiritual principle. For example, the burning incense symbolized the prayer of saints and intercession of the Mediator. Although the Old Testament ceremonial laws have expired and the judicial case laws are abrogated, they are still in the Word of God.

The ceremonial laws were added to the moral law to typify and prefigure the Lord Jesus Christ. They were given to the "church underage" so that the types and ordinances represented the person, work, and benefits that believers have in the Lord Jesus Christ. Those external ceremonial laws were given for worship at the place prescribed by God. In due time God appointed the place to worship, the temple of Jerusalem. With its destruction, the ceremonial laws are now abrogated because they were put aside by the completed work of the Lord Jesus Christ (Colossians 2:14-17; Ephesians 2:15-16).

The judicial case laws expired with the disestablishment of the Old Testament political state of Israel, as a church underage. Then what value are those judicial case laws to Christians in this present age? The Westminster Assembly used the terminology "general equity" in the application of those laws under the new covenant. Long before Westminster gave its counsel, John Calvin had said, "the form of their [the nation of Israel] judicial laws, although it had no other intent than how best to preserve that very love which is enjoined by God's eternal law, had something distinct from that precept of love. Therefore, as ceremonial laws could be abrogated while piety remained safe and unharmed, so too, when these judicial laws were taken away, the perpetual duties and precepts of love could still remain" (*Institutes of the Christian Religion*, 4.20.15). The Biblical principle of retributive justice (*lex talionis*) applies to all human government. The primary basis for that view is based on the biblical concept of natural law (i.e. Romans 2:14, 15).

The Word of God has not expired nor has it been abrogated. There are five biblical principles found in the Pentateuch that have a place in the lives of all New Testament Christians. A biblical principle is a fundamental truth of doctrine derived from the entire teaching of Scripture. These principles are established on the foundation of God's covenant relationship with His people of all ages. New Testament Christians will benefit from these godly principles if they will search the Scriptures and discover the truth found in the whole counsel of God.

The first principle is the agrarian way of life. A rural society based on agricultural production is the fundamental principle of the agrarian way of life. One of the most popular advocates of the agrarian way of life in modern times is Wendell Berry.

> We agrarians are involved in a hard, long, momentous contest, in which we are so far, and by a considerable margin, the losers. What we have undertaken to defend is the complex accomplishment of knowledge, cultural memory, skill, self-mastery, good sense, and fundamental decency—the high and indispensable art—for which

16. Looking Back

we probably can find no better name than 'good farming.' I mean farming as defined by agrarianism as opposed to farming as defined by industrialism: farming as the proper use and care of an "immeasurable gift." Mr. Berry explains his understanding of industrialism in relation to the agrarian way of life. "THE WAY OF INDUSTRIALISM is the way of the machine. To the industrial mind, a machine is not merely an instrument for doing work or amusing ourselves or making war; it is an explanation of the world and of life. Because industrialism cannot understand living things except as machines, and can grant them no value that is not utilitarian, it conceives of farming and forestry as forms of mining; it cannot use the land without abusing it." (*Orion Magazine*, Summer 2002, "The Agrarian Standard", by Wendell Berry)

There is every reason to believe that the agricultural enterprise was the dominant factor in God's plan to provide for His people. Without question the Hebrew institutions from the creation until the death of Moses were instrumental in producing an agricultural society. Man was created and placed in a perfect world that was perfectly agrarian (Genesis 2:15). God was perfectly able to create a city to place the man in, but God chose a garden for Adam to cultivate and keep. After the fall there was a change in the garden; However, Adam was still in a unique relationship to the ground (Genesis 3:17).

Agriculture and land are inseparable. A rural society seems to be favored by God. Cain began his life as an agrarian, but turned to urbanization which requires an industrial and commercial way of life (Genesis 4:2; 17). The earliest recorded history of cities found in the Word of God carried with it negative and sinful connotations (Genesis 11:4). God established laws to protect the land for agricultural use, but not for cities (Leviticus 25:25-30). A rural and agricultural society is more suited to ignore class distinctions found in urban populations.

The agrarian principle has merit today just as it did when God created Adam and put him in the garden. Think hypothetically one moment. If every family in this country had a small garden and worked that small garden, it would have a radical effect in every area of life. The concept of agrarianism was and still is the principle of God's provision from the ground, not from the commercial grocery store. It would promote a biblical work ethic which is commanded in the 4th commandment: "Six days you shall labor and do all your work" (Exodus 20:9). Urbanization, commercialization, and industrialization, is a breeding ground for a discontent society because there is no covenantal connection between them and God's provision for human existence.

The second principle I draw from Old Testament Hebrew institutions is relative to the practice of foreign policy and trade. In the early days of Israel, she did not try to expand her trade and commerce by entering into covenants with foreign nations. Phoenicians came to trade with the Hebrews, but the Hebrews did not build a naval force to reciprocate. God warned His people not to enter into a covenant with foreigners (Exodus 34:12-16). International trade leads to international obligations. The Lord warned the Israelites not to borrow from other nations (Deuteronomy 15:6). To observe the laws of foreign nations was detestable to the Lord. The entire history of Israel from the time of Solomon until the destruction of the Temple in 586 B.C. is a testimony of what happened to God's people who entered into agreements, trade or military, with other nations. Foreign trade has the potential to denigrate the value of the land and the labor of the citizens who own the land and produce the goods. The principle application of Hebrew institutions relative to foreign policy and trade in our present age is self evident.

16. Looking Back

The third principle is found in the Old Testament Hebrew ordinances regulating the economic financial transactions. The Old Testament legislation was specific relative to the regulating land ownership, monetary transactions, and indebtedness. God owns all the land on this earth. God created land and while we are alive God allows us to use the land. We are allowed to live on it and use it to provide for our needs. The Old Testament Hebrew ordinances regulated the disposition of land (Leviticus 25:23-34). Money was transferred between various parties by means of precious metals such as gold and silver. The way to determine the value was by weight and the use of scales. Honesty was not merely a virtue, it was commanded by God (Leviticus 19:35; Deuteronomy 25:13-16). Indebtedness was not a sin, but it was regulated by God's ordinances. Money could be loaned but not with interest except to the foreigner (Deuteronomy23:19-20). Debt cancellation was the means to protect the poor from a life time of suffering. God called on the Israelites to open the hand wide to the poor, even if the year of debt cancellation was at hand (Deuteronomy 15:7-11). The principle still stands: compassion, but not communism.

The fourth principle was the military policy of Israel. Two outstanding features found in the Pentateuch:

No empire expansion
No colonization

A covenant is an agreement based on stipulations and promises between the two parties. The philosophical principle that necessitates the covenant concept between equals is the sinful disposition to engage in war. Israel was not commanded to have a standing army like the other nations so that once a year they might engage in war. It was normal for other nations to fight for land and conquer for reasons other than just war.

God has given us one whole chapter that defines the principles governing warfare (Deuteronomy 20:1-20).

Three philosophical categories that deal with the concept we call war:

> Activism – All war is permissible. Unbending obedience to the civil magistrate. "My country right or wrong."
>
> Pacifism – All war is wrong. No involvement in war. Anabaptists and Mennonites.
>
> Selectivism – Some war is justified, therefore the just war theory is legitimate.

God created everything including a rational creature, called man. God established a peace treaty which we call a covenant. The man desired to assume God's role which violated God's original covenant. When man broke the covenant it was like breaking a peace treaty. With the peace treaty broken, naturally God had every right and obligation to declare war. God had every right to exercise individual, international, and even cosmological justice. It was properly a holy war and it was a just war. The question before us is this: Does man have the right and authority to declare war?

Let me make a prefatory statement before we engage any further in this discussion. The human race cannot blame God or Satan for that matter, for the crisis we call war. Sinful man is responsible for war. The sinful man-centered desire for self preservation, self interest, and self esteem will inevitability lead to war. Nations are unjust and ungodly because the people of the nation are unjust and ungodly. The inspired proverbial doctrine is defined in these terms: "Righteousness exalts a nation, but sin is a disgrace to any people" (Proverbs 14:34).

16. Looking Back

I believe that activism is a sin against God and mankind. Dr. R. L. Dabney describes it in more graphic terms. "Unprovoked war is the most monstrous secular crime that can be committed: it is at once the greatest of evils and includes the worst forms of robbery and murder" (*Dabney's Systematic Theology*, by R. L. Dabney, pg. 403).

Although pacifism has noble and generous goals, it is not conceivable or possible in a post fall world. The inevitability of war requires a biblical response to war. I believe the biblical response may be classified under the category of just war.

The preface to any war is the offer of peace (Deuteronomy 20:10). If the enemy refuses the covenant, then war may be the only alternative. The Word of God does not prescribe war, nor does it proscribe war.

I believe the biblical principles of war have been largely ignored in the history of Western Civilization. I also believe those principles provide guidelines that would be more sensible and productive toward peace on this planet.

The fifth and most significance principle was the establishment of a graded judiciary to govern the people. The nation of Israel consisted of twelve tribes. Their religious, social, and civil lives were particular to them because of God's covenant design. God's grace was evident in His covenant promises to His children. Their King and Governor was the Lord God almighty. They were joined together which means they were confederated as a particular people by a sovereign monarch. The Lord then appointed Moses to select qualified men to judge the people (Exodus 18:21-26). Eventually, the people turned away from God's government, in favor of man's government (1 Samuel 8:5). It proved to be the destruction of a nation. The application of God's plan is closely related to a confederated republic. Each tribe, state, etc has its own leadership, but is confederated with other tribes, states, etc for common purposes.

17. Death

And when I saw Him, I fell at His feet as dead. But He laid His right hand on me, saying to me, "Do not be afraid; I am the First and the Last. I am He who lives, and was dead, and behold, I am alive forevermore. Amen. And I have the keys of Hades and of Death.

Revelation 1:17-18

There are times when death is difficult to explain. Christians will find more answers in the Bible than any other source. In this little exercise, I will ask some questions about death and let the Bible answer those questions.

How does the Bible describe death?

> Returning to dust (Genesis 3:19)
> A harvesting (Job 5:26)
> Like the vanishing of a cloud (James 4:14)
> Departing this life (Philippians 1:23)
> The Last Enemy (1 Corinthians 15:26, Revelation 21:4)
> What is the cause of death? (Roman 5:12)

Who ordained death?

> Psalm 104:29
> Deuteronomy 32:39
> 1 Samuel 2:6

What are the major characteristics of death?

> Universal (Hebrews 9:27, Ecclesiastes 9:3)
> Inevitable (Psalm 89:48)
> Uncertain of its time (James 4:14, Proverbs 27:1)

From the pen of a Puritan: "Nothing is so sure as death, and nothing so uncertain as the time. I may be too old to live, I can never be too young to die; I will therefore live every hour, as if I were to die the next."

Why do people fear death?

>Lack of confidence in the one who has power over death (Hebrews 2:14, 15)
>
>Attachment to the world (Mark 10:17-22)
>
>Lack of hope and assurance of God's saving grace (2 Corinthians 13:5)

How should one prepare for death?

>Spiritual preparation (Hebrews 11:7)
>Believe on Christ (John 11:25)

What does the Bible say about the soul after the body dies?

>It leaves the body (Ecclesiastes 12:7)
>Death ends the desire for earthly endeavors (Ecclesiastes 9:10)

Since death finds its way to all men, we should examine what the Bible says about two classes of men - the righteous and the wicked.

What does the Bible say about the death of the righteous?

>The righteous man is full of peace at death (Isaiah 57:1-2)

17. Death

> The righteous man is full of hope at death (Proverbs 14:32)
> The righteous man will not fear death (Psalm 23:4)
> The righteous man's death is precious in the sight of God (Psalm 116:15)
> The righteous man finds that death is gain (Philippians 1:21)

What does the Bible say about the death of the wicked?

> The wicked man has no hope (Proverbs 11:7)
> The wicked man's death is marked by terror (Job 18:11)
> The wicked man's death is like that of an animal (Psalm 49:14)
> The wicked man's death is followed by punishment (Luke 16:24)

The question is often asked, what happens to the disembodied soul until the resurrection when the new body is joined to the soul? Theologians refer to this as the intermediate state. The Westminster Assembly explained the intermediate state in these terms.

> The bodies of men after death return to dust, and see corruption; but their souls (which neither die nor sleep), immediately return to God who gave them. . .where they behold the face of God in light and glory, waiting for the full redemption of their bodies. . .and the souls of the wicked are cast into hell. . .Besides theses two places for souls separated from their bodies, the Scripture acknowledgeth none. (*Westminster Confession of Faith*, 32.1)

The Present Truth

Death is the gateway to a final destination for all rational creatures. If there is a fear factor it is not death itself; it is the destination after the event known as death. The Bible declares that every rational creature will have an everlasting home, either heaven or hell. If heaven is your eternal home, words will not describe the peace, joy, and rest for the residents of that place. If hell is your eternal home, words will not describe the war, sorrow, and unending labor for the residents in that place.

18. Brief Comments

A Christian Belief System
Christian Civil Affairs
Truth in a Nutshell
World and Life Views
Humanism
Secularism
Individualism
Talking About History
Timely Questions
Trials and Temptations
Those Golden Years
Confessional Christianity
The Faithful Minister
Learning to Learn
Arminianism
Calvinism
Classical Apologetics
What is a Cult?

CHRISTIAN BELIEF SYSTEM

J. Gresham Machen said, "The absence of doctrinal teaching and preaching is certainly one of the causes for the present lamentable ignorance in the church." Dr. Machen went on to say, "Doctrine is intellectual, and Christians are generally anti-intellectual. Doctrine is ivory tower philosophy, and they scorn ivory towers. . . It is a fundamental, theoretical mistake of practical men to think that they can be merely practical, for practice is always the practice of some theory" (*Education, Christianity and the State,* J. Gresham Machen, p.169). It is sad but true that many churchmen think that teaching and preaching from a sound theological foundation is theoretical.

A theological belief system (and everyone has a theological belief system) will effect how one thinks, acts, and performs in the world we live. Modernist believe that theology is like a novelty shop where one may find all sorts of unusual goodies, but often these novelties are disguised as the real thing. Truth and accuracy in interpretation will expose the false covering, but it requires hard work and patience. The evangelical church in our country has been plagued with a smorgasbord of theology and philosophy for several generations and we need not expect to see a correction come easily or quickly.

The mind understands according to the perspectives and yes the presuppositions of a total belief system. For instance, I cannot gather any knowledge and sort out that knowledge in my mind without bringing many other ideas, facts, and data in the full picture. To claim to be able to do otherwise will cause some flirting with ancient Greek philosophies like Gnosticism and Stoicism. Somehow they claim to obtain secret knowledge to aid in their Christian growth. Any such idea is foreign to Holy Scripture.

We derive our theological system from the Bible, but we are not the Bible. We are fallible human beings who interpret the Bible using all the resources that God gives in this fallen world. Our theology is not a belief system without the influence of common grace, but Scripture must regulate it as we are enabled by the Holy Spirit to discover the nature and character of God.

CHRISTIAN CIVIL AFFAIRS

The civil responsibility of the Christian is found in Paul's letters to the Romans. It is there that the inspired apostle said of the Gentiles "who show the work of the law written in their hearts, their conscience also bearing witness…"(Romans 2:15). The *jus natura* (a system of natural

18. Brief Comments

law) calls every human being before the cosmic court to answer the charges of the Judge of the Universe. The *jus natura* is an allusion to the essential nature of man and explains why human beings have familial governments that collectively form governments in a larger society. This is nothing more than a Christian living in a civil world.

The civil affairs of men are matters that concern the sphere of ethics and morality. Since the law is written on the heart, the law of God is binding on the civil magistrate (government) as well as the Christian. Obedience or disobedience to the law of God finally finds its end in justice. The basis of justice is authority. Moses makes the point that "You shall appoint judges and officers in all your gates, which the Lord your God gives you, according to your tribes, and they shall judge the people with just judgment" (Deut. 16:18).

The Bible does not explicitly mandate a civil form of government. However natural right theory, so popular among the social contract advocates, is anti-biblical. The political theory that gives the king divine right, although more sensible than the social contract theory is a weakened view of civil politics. The New Testament does not say obey the king, but it does say submit to the governing authorities. The question is whether or not obedience is absolute and final when the governing authority speaks?

Peter and the other apostles were charged not to teach the doctrine of Christ, but Peter understood that there was a higher law to be obeyed. For that reason Scripture tells us "We ought to obey God rather than men" (Acts 5:29). When Christians were commanded by the governing authorities in Rome to worship idols, the Christians disobeyed. Christians are not bound in conscience to obey against the clear teaching of Scripture. Christians are commanded to render to Caesar the things that are Caesar's and to God the things that are God's.

The failure of the church to teach natural law is one of the primary reasons that prevent Christians from defending the truth of the law written on stone by the finger of God. Christians have the responsibility to teach the culture natural law principles.

TRUTH IN A NUTSHELL

What is truth? Theologians and philosophers in all ages wrestle with this question. Truth is that which is in agreement to that which is represented. Truth corresponds to reality, so you might say that truth is that which conforms to fact or reality. However we live in a postmodern world that declares all objective real truth is dead. Dr. Os Guinness observes that "in a postmodern world, the question is not 'Is it true?' but rather 'Whose truth is it?' and 'Which power stands to gain?'"

Christians have the Bible and are enabled by the Holy Spirit to understand biblical truth. Jesus manifestly explained how unbelievers do not understand biblical truth (John 8:43-47). The Bible speaks for itself; "The sum of Thy word is truth" (Psalm 119:160). Christians ought to be affected by that truth. "Thou are near, O Lord, and all Thy commandments are truth" (Psalm 119:151). Moral truth will affect every part of life. Moral truth is rooted in the integrity of God; therefore truth is an attribute of God which God has chosen to share with His creatures.

The Bible teaches that there is saving power in truth. "But as for me, my prayer is to Thee, O Lord, at an acceptable time; O God, in the greatness of Thy lovingkindness answer me with Thy saving truth" (Psalm 69:13).

Truth serves as a point of reference for Christians. Jonathan Edwards explains truth this way: "After all that has been said and done, the only adequate definition of truth is the agreement of our ideas with existence." He later defines existence (ultimate existence) as a synonym for God. Therefore since truth is from the essence of God everything that comes from God is truth. God is the point of reference for

Christians. It is the duty of all Christians to think about God's truth. The Bible tells us to take "every thought captive to the obedience of Christ" (2 Corinthians 10:5). Today Christians are being lulled to sleep by the charm of Satan's lies. Satan's deceptive tricks try to convince Christians that truth is relative and there is no difference between truth and error. Wake up Christians! It is the last hour.

WORLD AND LIFE VIEWS

The church is confronted and seduced by all sorts of "isms" in our modern culture. An "ism" is, of course, any particular world and life view. The letters "ism" attached to the end of a word, simply represent a philosophy of life or the way a person thinks about the world or how one relates to the world.

There are too many "isms" to enumerate, but just to give you an idea here are a few: Secularism, humanism, materialism, consumerism, pragmatism, positivism, pluralism, relativism, hedonism, individualism, narcissism, victimizationalism skepticism, and the list goes on. Christians must ask how these "isms" relate to and affect Christianity.

First, Christians must realize that any "ism" (world and life view) must be fundamentally rooted in the supernaturalism of Christianity. Christians cannot adopt a world and life view that is not in agreement with the belief and existence in a personal God and the existence of the real order of nature in the providence of God.

Secondly, Christianity is characterized by a philosophy of truth. Truth is not relative! God is not confused, nor can God contradict Himself. God is at perfect peace with the purity and essence of truth in His mind. One of the chief rivals in modern Christianity is the idea that truth is relative. Classical Christianity rejects such a thought!

Christians should have some knowledge of how the various "isms" affect them corporately as a church and individually as Christians. It is the duty of Christians to formulate a world and life view that places the God they worship in the centerpiece of their thinking. Theism is the fundamental world and life view of the Christian religion. Theism is the world and life view that acknowledges our relationship to God in a personal way and further that God's nature and character is what is claimed in the Word of God.

HUMANISM

The Renaissance of the 14th through the 16th century brought about a revival of "human" learning and a return to the classics. The rebirth of interest in classical literature and language along with the desire to revitalize culture and intellectual pursuits is said to be the source of religious humanism. Religious humanism found its way in the church through such thinkers as Erasmus, Arminius, and Locke. They believed that man was basically good and had great confidence in the power of education. These thinkers saw human rights as the vehicle to make good men, better men.

Over the course of time, religious humanism has evolved and has now become known as secular humanism. The American Humanist Association along with other humanist organizations teach that "Humanism asserts that the nature of the universe depicted by modern science makes unacceptable any supernatural or cosmic guarantees of human values." Humanism is inseparably connected to Secularism. Humanism is an enemy of Christianity!

Francis Schaeffer, an evangelical theologian and philosopher, said that "humanism intends to beat to death the [Christian] base which made our culture possible." Schaeffer is correct! The modern humanist has a goal to destroy Christian ethics, morals, and values. They embrace the doctrine of man and deny the doctrine of God. The modern humanist believes that the supreme dignity for man is found in man himself. An ancient Greek philosopher named Protagoras has given the modern humanist a motto: "Man, the measure." Protagoras believed that man was the measure of all things.

Humanism has had a tremendous influence on the church. The impact is so great that Christians often embrace tenets of Humanism, even while they remain unaware of the danger of humanism. How should Christians respond to this powerful world view. Christians are the salt of the earth [and] the light of the world. "Let your light shine before men in such a way that they may see your good works, and glorify your Father who is in heaven." (Matthew 5:16).

SECULARISM

The western world can boast of an abundance of worldviews. The generality of the worldviews in our nation do not find their roots in religion, but rather in philosophy. It is particularly dangerous to believe that the United States is a Christian nation. Such thinking promotes the idea that the world views espoused by the majority of the citizens of this nation are rooted in Christianity.

Secularism is a worldview that encompasses many worldviews and is rapidly ascending in popularity. The western world has experienced a rise in secularism, as a worldview, during the 20th century. Secularism is the most influential philosophy in the western world. This is important for Christians to understand, because Secularism is in direct opposition to Christianity. The tragedy, is that during the last decade of the 20th century, Secularism is being widely accepted by Christians.

The root of the word Secularism is the word secular. The word secular describes the here and now. "Live for today, because there may not be a tomorrow," so says the Secularist.

The aestheticians, the world of media (especially news media), and the literary artists of our age are overwhelmingly committed to Secularism. There is nothing wrong with secular; it simply defines the present time. The conflict with Christianity is when the secular claims to exclude the eternal. Christians are interested in the present world, but their primary concern ought to be the eternal. The Bible teaches that Christians must be involved in the secular, but Christians cannot deny the sacred. Secularism excludes the eternal. Secularism not only conflicts with Christianity, but by excluding the eternal, it rejects Christianity.

The secular is inseparably connected to the sacred or the eternal. The danger for Christians is to profess hope for the eternal, yet embrace Secularism and therefore reject the hope of the eternal. "For man goes to his eternal home while mourners go about in the street" (Ecclesiastes 12:5).

INDIVIDUALISM

Although individualism has a rich history, there has been a tendency to subsume individualism as an integral part of various classical philosophies. Modern man has taken this world view and exploited it, especially the left wing politically correct crowd, so that individualism stands at the forefront among the contemporary world views.

The Greek city/state (the polis), the Roman ideal, the Renaissance, the Reformation, Modernity and now Post-modernity have all faced a certain degree of individualism. My thesis is that although individualism is a moving force within Christianity, it is not a Christian world view.

Individualism embraces other world views such as secularism, humanism, pragmatism, and consumerism. Christians are certainly secular, human, pragmatic, and consumers. However, a Christian world view places the importance on the sacred rather than the secular, the divine

18. Brief Comments

rather than the human, the truth rather than expedience, and the good life rather than the happy life. The Christian world view places the emphasis on the sovereignty of God rather than the power of the individual.

Why have Christians rejected the sovereignty of God and favored the power of individual preferences? There are a number of factors. First, Christians have rejected orthodox Christian doctrine and theology. Secondly and related to the first, Christians have lost their passion for investigating truth. Thirdly and significantly, 20th century Christians are interpreting the Bible without considering the contextual, cultural, and historical factors. For example, the average person would say, "I have my individual rights as a citizen of these United (really un-united) States." The idea is that in a democracy the people rule. Throughout most of the history of the Bible and the history of the church many people have been under some form of monarchy. The individual had rights only if the sovereign monarch granted such rights.

The Christian world view is the only world view that grants individual rights (de facto). Christians are the only people who are really and eternally given individual rights and at the same time Christians are under the rule of a sovereign monarch, the Lord Jesus Christ. Jesus said, "you shall know the truth, and the truth shall make you free" (John 8:32). A Christian is one who is adopted into the family of God and is an individual sibling among many siblings. It is the duty of all Christians to reject the philosophy of individualism and accept the sovereignty of God as the ruling principle in life.

TALKING ABOUT HISTORY

Webster's Dictionary defines history as "the branch of knowledge dealing with past events" and/or "the record of past events especially in connection with the human race." The generally accepted definition of history is contrary to a Christian world and life view. Dr. Rousas Rushdonny points out that "history as it comes from the hand of God has a preordained meaning and direction, and it moves to a purpose neither decreed by man or conducive to man's sin. As a result, man is in revolt against history. Man pits against history the imagination of his fallen heart" (*Foundation of Social Order*, Rousas Rushdonny, pg. 9).

The English word "history" has its origin in the Greek word *historeo* and it is used one time in the Bible. The apostle Paul records in Galatians that he "went up to Jerusalem to become acquainted with Cephas [Peter]." *Historeo* translated "acquainted" literally means that Paul went to "visit" (become acquainted) with Peter. The word history means to inquire or examine something; literally to be acquainted with something. When sinful historians visit, inquire, or examine an event or person of the past, the interpreted result may be erroneous. The only true accurate history is the Bible.

The historical truth from Scripture is either descriptive or normative. Whatever the Bible described actually happened. The mandates in Scripture are historically normal, but sinners despise them.

The present crisis in the church is a result of the ignorance of historical truth and rebellion against the God of history. The lack of interest in the philosophy of history is the primary contributing factor. As George Hegel said, the history of philosophy is "the thoughtful consideration of it" [history]. The first thoughtful consideration is the inspired history of Holy Scripture. The second thoughtful consideration is the use of intelligent laws of discourse to interpret secular history.

Unbelievers are not able to consistently pursue the truth of history. It must be left to the Christians.

TIMELY QUESTIONS

18. Brief Comments

Theology, doctrine, and truth were landmarks of the evangelical church in past centuries. Holy Scripture was the means to measure the worship and work of the church. Sola Scriptura, Scripture alone, was the absolute universal standard. Today those things that work best or more specifically those things that seem best at the particular time and situation measure the worship and work of the church, to a large degree. The evangelical church has moved away from a God-centered ministry and has adopted a man-centered ministry. All factors considered, the evangelical church is at the edge of a cliff, but the church is not in a maze. We can see the way to safe ground. We need to ask ourselves these questions:

> Do we resort to the Holy Scripture to learn the work and worship of the church?
>
> Do we have a passion for truth, especially for an understanding of God's creative work and redemptive plan?
>
> Do we seek the glory of God as the zenith of our existence?
>
> Are we a holy people?
>
> Have we done all things according to God's Word?

There are other questions we should ask, but those questions are sufficient to chew on for the present time. I not only want the evangelical church to survive; I want it to thrive, but not at the risk of hypocritical behavior and heretical deviations. Hypocrisy is the representation of something that does not exist. Heresy is when one makes a choice that leads to factions and divisions. Hypocrisy and heresy will push the church over the edge.

Charles Spurgeon once said, "The reason why some churches do not prosper is, because they have not done things according to God's Word."

TRIALS AND TEMPTATIONS

During a testimony meeting one Christian lady stood up and said, "I'm always blessed by the words 'it came to pass.' When I'm upset by troubles, I go to the Bible and I never read very far before the Bible says 'it came to pass.' Then I say bless the Lord it didn't come to stay, it came to pass." When Christians face trials in this life they must remember that trials are not here to stay.

Christians face all kinds of trials. When trials come "consider it all joy." Trials are necessary for Christian growth and maturity. The purpose of trials is to prove the Christian's profession of faith.

Christians often react to trials zealously or fearlessly which often leads one into temptation. Jesus said pray "lest you enter into temptation." A trial such as sickness, emotional trauma, or financial disaster may turn into a temptation to question God or turn to unbelief.

The source of temptation is not God, because "God cannot be tempted by evil, nor does He tempt anyone." The sinful nature of man tends to blame sinful behavior on others. The source of temptation is man for the Bible says, "each one is tempted when, by his own evil desire, he is dragged away and enticed" (James 1:14). Satan is involved with temptation because he has the power of deceit to use against the believer. The Bible does not say Christians are tempted by someone else's evil desire, not even the Devil's evil desire, but the evil desire of the sinner. Trials come from an outside source, but the persuasion to yield to temptation comes from within.

18. Brief Comments

Temptation grows and brings forth sin like a seed brings forth a plant. If the plant grows to its full stature the result is misery, pain and ultimately death (James 1:15).

The remedy is confession, repentance, forgiveness and reconciliation. "Prove yourselves doers of the word, and not merely hearers who delude themselves" (James 1:22). Pray for the Holy Spirit to enable you to be "doers of the word."

THOSE GOLDEN YEARS

"I'm a senior citizen" or "I'm retired" often refers to those golden years of life. It is those clichés that fail to reflect the joy of those golden years. You may feel old at forty or young at eighty, but only you can determine the value of a mature life. Although truth is not relative, there are many aspects of life that can be measured relative to something else. Obviously aging is relative to those circumstances that accompany a mature life.

The Bible has much to say about old age, but in a world that looks only at the fast lane, there is not much attention given to the scriptural principles to guide those into the sunset of life.

Unfortunately the first thoughts on aging are generally negative. The Bible addresses issues like vision, strength, and vigor. The story of Issac losing his eyesight in has later years is a good example of how age takes its toll on life. David lost his strength in the twilight of his life. Christians are unique because they may call on God for health, strength and life. The Psalmist said, "Do not cast me off in the time of old age; Do not forsake me when my strength fails" (Psalm 71:9, NJKV). There is a kind of urgency in this prayer, but the Psalmist was not ashamed to ask for help because it is during the latter years that we especially need the grace of God to keep the body up and going. Charles Spurgeon has rightly said, "It is not unnatural or improper for a man who sees old age coming upon him to pray for special grace, and special strength, to enable him to meet with that he cannot ward off and what he cannot but dread."

The wisdom literature of Scripture (Job through Song of Solomon) reflects the attitude that should accompany old age. "I said age should speak, and multitude of years should teach wisdom" (Job 32:7, NKJV). The failure to respect maturity in life is a mark of declining values in cultures around the world. Young people should have respect for their elders and explore the vast wealth in the senior mind. Rehoboam made a fatal error when he rejected the counsel of the elders of Israel. He chose his young friends to counsel him and in the end the bad counsel of the young men was an instrument of destruction for the nation.

Old age is desirable. The story is told of a king who became irritated by his court jester and in a sudden rage of wrath the king sentenced the court jester to death. Then realizing he had decreed this awful thing said to the court jester: "In consideration of your faithful services, I will permit you to select the manner in which you prefer to die." The court jester instantly answered, "I select to die of old age."

History is replete with examples of people doing great works in the golden years of life. Moses was eighty when God called him to lead the children of Israel out of Egypt. Phillips Brooks was a great and powerful preacher at eighty years of age. Benjamin Franklin wrote his autobiography when he was over eighty.

The gift of seeing the sunset of life at an old age is a privilege and joy. It is a great privilege to share the wisdom from a chest of life experiences. The joy of sharing that wisdom with the next generation is the way to walk into the sunset in peace.

CONFESSIONAL CHRISTIANITY

18. Brief Comments

A confession is simply the acknowledgment or disclosure of something, such as the acknowledgment of a known particular sin. In a more positive sense, a confession is the admission and profession of a particular belief. A confession is a statement of belief made personally and publicly. One way to confess a belief system is to use a creed, such as the Apostles' or Nicene Creed.

The concept of confession is particularly important to Christians. A person cannot be a Christian without confession. When the soul of man is renewed by the power of the Holy Spirit, confession of sin is essential to conversion. A sinner saved by grace must then publicly confess faith in the Lord Jesus Christ. For example Peter confessed saying, "You are the Christ, the Son of the living God" (Matthew 16:16). If there is no confession there is no Christianity.

The composition of confessions has a rich history in the church. We have the Apostles' Creed, Nicene Creed, and the Athanasian Creed, which are ecumenical creeds. The Roman Catholic Church, the Eastern Orthodox Church, and the Protestant Churches have their individual creeds. The creeds are the confessional statements of what those particular churches believe.

The 16th century Reformation saw an outpouring of confessional statements to help direct the church toward a sense of uniformity. Unfortunately the sinful heart tends to idolize the confession. A confession is not inspired or infallible. Confessional documents were formulated for the express purpose of giving the Reformed churches a distinctive and identifiable doctrine and form of worship.

THE FAITHFUL MINISTER

Like the swirl of an eddy many churches in this country spin in disarray while the main stream of society follows a false hope sinful curriculum. Is there any hope for faithful

Christians? The answer is yes! "Do not fear what you are about to suffer. Behold, the devil is about to cast some of you into prison, that you may be tested, and you will have tribulation ten days. Be faithful until death, and I will give you the crown of life" (Revelation 2:10).

The contemporary church is under the influence of ungodly cultural norms. A variety of ungodly worldviews fills the mind of Christians because ministers are not faithful to the Word of God. The faithful prophets in the Old Testament were the minority. Although there have been times of revival, the faithful ministers in the New Testament church are also a minority. The most faithful ministers suffered the greater persecution.

Jonathan Edwards is a good example of a faithful minister. His congregation removed him from the pulpit in Northampton because of his faithful ministry. He moved to a small outpost at Stockbridge. In 1753 he wrote a letter to another faithful minister who also suffered persecution. Edwards said, "As to my own circumstances, I am still meeting with trouble, and expect no other as long as I live in this world. Some great men have mightily opposed my continuing the missionary at Stockbridge, and have taken occasion abundantly to reproach me, and endeavor my removal."

Edwards ended the letter with these words of encouragement. "Let us thus endeavor to help one another (though at a great distance) in traveling through this wide wilderness, that we may have the more joyful meeting in the land of rest, when we have finished our weary pilgrimage."

We are all ministers because ministers are servants (slaves) of the Most High God. May it be that the faithful will hear "Well done, good and faithful slave; you were faithful with a few things, I will put you in charge of many things, enter into the joy of your master."

18. Brief Comments

LEARNING TO LEARN

Thousands of sermons, teaching sessions, seminars, and lectures on the Christian religion and western philosophy in general have fallen upon my ears over the past fifty years. I've consumed hundreds of books and devoted the last one third of my life in study and research relative to the Christian religion. God has graced me with an eternal relationship with Him through the Lord Jesus Christ, by the power of the Holy Spirit. Until this day, God has given me an able body and sound mind to devote myself to learning more about myself, others, and especially God, the triune God, the Father, the Son and the Holy Spirit. Even so, I find myself learning to learn.

Moses prayed to God and said, "Teach us [the children of God] to number our days That we may present to Thee a heart of wisdom" (Psalm 90:12). Today I counted my days on this earth. They are 23,556. Easy! However, to present to God a heart of wisdom is not easy. Wisdom is not the same thing as knowledge, but wisdom is not possible without knowledge. Francis Turretin quotes Suidas saying that wisdom is "the learning and the skillful use of contemplation, knowledge, and recognition."

Now I will go to the crux of the subject in the form of a question. Does the knowledge of myself, others, and God match the number of days I've been given to acquire such knowledge? My head drops in humility as I realize just how many of those days that have been squandered in pleasures, self indulgence, and self gratification. Issac Watts wrote a book for children and youth on the subject, which is also the title of the book, *The Improvement of the Mind*. It was published in 1833 and re-printed in 1998. I have valued its content ever since my first reading of it. It is a book about how to acquire and use knowledge that will be an aid to make one wise. In the preface Watts gives the reader a summary of the book. First it "lays down remarks and rules how we may attain useful knowledge ourselves; and the second, how we may best communicate it to others." Christians ought to be learning to learn. Knowledge is not acquired by speculative osmosis. Watts saw the need to teach children how to learn. Watts wrote *The Improvement of the Mind* so that young people might "seek the cultivation of their own understandings (notice the plural) in the early days of life." Watts goes on to give sage advice to young people. "Perhaps, they may find something here which may awake a latent genius, and direct the studies of a willing mind. Perhaps it may point out to a student now and then what may employ the most useful labours of his thoughts and accelerate his diligence in the momentous enquiries."

The brain is a bodily organ that acquires knowledge in this physical world. The brain will turn to dust. The mind is the metaphysical entity that acquires knowledge. The mind is a component of the soul and will remain forever. The renewing of the mind by the power of the Holy Spirit will create a desire to understand the purpose, mission, and ministry of the church. "None of the wicked shall understand, but the wise shall understand" (Daniel 12:10).

ARMINIANISM

Christian adherents embrace a variety of worldviews. The majority of Christians in America call themselves evangelical. Evangelicalism describes a broad category of Protestant Christians primarily consisting of two doctrinal worldviews commonly known as Arminianism and Calvinism.

Arminianism, like any other theological system, has a wide range of doctrinal diversity, but its roots can be traced to the teaching of Jacobus Arminius (Jakob Hermandszoon) who was a Dutch theologian in the 17th century. The first generation students of Jacobus Arminius protested against the system of doctrine taught by the followers of John Calvin. The controversy was settled at the Synod of Dort (1618-1619) held

18. Brief Comments

in the Netherlands, which concluded that the Arminians were not orthodox. The synod condemned the Arminians and removed them from their pulpits. The synod decided against Arminian doctrine, but subsequent theologians did not. The system of doctrine developed by John Wesley was Arminian and in fact his movement was known as "Arminianism on fire." There has been a massive spill over of certain tenets of Arminianism into most evangelical churches.

What do Arminians believe? In the 17th century an assessment would have been relatively simple, but in the 20th century the divisions within Arminianism are multiple. Millard Erickson, an evangelical theologian, has this definition: "Arminianism holds that God's decision to give salvation to certain persons and not to others is based upon his foreknowledge of who will believe. It also includes the idea that genuinely regenerated [born again] people can lose their salvation; [And] often has a less serious view of human depravity than does Calvinism."

Closing arguments are not in order! It is not my purpose here to explain all the technicalities of Arminianism. The purpose is to inform the readers that Arminianism is the majority report among evangelical Christians. If Arminianism is wrong, most of evangelical Christianity is wrong.

CALVINISM

John Calvin gave the Reformation (the Protestant church) a definitive and systematic statement in the *Institutes of the Christian Religion*. John Calvin was the leading thinker and theologian in the 16th century Reformation.

Although John Calvin was a mere man, but an extraordinary theologian to say the least, he was also fallible. However, his theological mistakes are negligible compared to the volume, intensity, and depth of his theological endeavors. Calvin was not only a theologian; he was a philosopher, church doctor, and economist. As one historian has said, "all Americans should know Calvin, because Calvinism is Capitalism."

Calvinism is a Christian worldview that is best known for its theological system. Calvin's original writings, copious for sure, are not that difficult to systematize and understand. The students of Calvinism, especially in the 20th century, complicated the massive work of this reformer, but Calvinism in a nutshell is simply an emphasis on the sovereignty of God.

One of the great criticisms of the Calvinistic doctrine is the sovereignty of God in the salvation of men. Read Ephesians 1:3-12 for the biblical teaching on the subject of predestination. However, notice Calvin's own words. "What else can account for the fact that predestination is a veritable sea of scandals except for our curiosity of forwardness? Here the point at issue is the secret judgment of God, whose glory is such that if men come too near, their minds must be not only stunned and stupefied but completely consumed by it" (*Concerning Scandals*, by John Calvin, p. 52).

Church historians would recognize St. Augustine, Martin Luther, John Calvin, and Jonathan Edwards as some of the most influential men in the history of the church. If that proposition is true, then the theological system known as Calvinism must be worthy of investigation because they believed the fundamental tenets of Calvinism. This is particularly true relative to the doctrine of God's sovereignty in salvation. Calvinism has stood the test of time throughout the history of the Protestant church. The real test for any theological system is the Holy Scripture. If Calvinism aligns with Scripture, then it is the Protestant worldview!

Theodore Beza, Calvin's biographer, said, "Having been an observer of Calvin's life for sixteen years, I may with perfect right testify that we have in this man a most beautiful example of a truly Christian life and death, which it is easy to calumniate, but difficult to imitate." Prof. Dorner writes:

18. Brief Comments

"Calvin was...lovely in social life, full of tender sympathy and faithfulness to friends, yielding and forgiving toward personal offences...."

CLASSICAL APOLOGETICS

Apologetics in the context of the Christian religion has both a positive and negative dimension. Positively the Christian apologist proves theism. Negatively the Christian apologist answers the charges of atheism. In both cases there is a logical progression for the apologist. He may find someone who believes that there is a God, but there is not a **triune** God. In another case a person may not believe that God exists, so the starting point is to prove theism. The logical progression is to lead someone to a clearer, but never fully clear, understanding of the nature and character of God. Apologetics can not and will not save anyone.

Classical apologetics is the minority report among conservative Reformed churches. However, it is called classical apologetics because the church used classical arguments throughout its history to prove the existence of God. Athanasius, Augustine, Anselm, Aquinas, John Calvin, Jonathan Edwards, B. B. Warfield and John Gerstner are a few examples of classical apologists using classical arguments. Then there were Southern Presbyterian giants like R. L. Dabney and J. H. Thornwell who were classical apologists. The most notable Southern Presbyterian to use the classical proofs was Francis Beatty.

The classical arguments for the existence of God consist of, but are not limited to the cosmological argument that answers the question: Where did the world come from? The teleological argument explains the origin of order and purpose in the world. The ontological argument states that there is a perfect being, self sufficient, and absolutely independent of creation. Other arguments may include the anthropological and moral arguments. The rational common ground among rational creatures is the rational starting point for intellectual discourse.

A classical apologist is one who sees the apologetical enterprise as a significant part of his world and life view. Since apologetics is necessarily connected with ones thinking and learning process, apologetics will have a wide influence on any Christian ministry. The theory of knowledge is inseparable from the practice of apologetics.

WHAT IS A CULT?

Webster's Encyclopedic Unabridged Dictionary of the English Language has the meaning of the word "cult" divided into seven different nuances. First, a cult is described as "a particular system of religious worship, especially with reference to its rites and ceremonies." If that definition is used, then some people might refer to Christianity as a cult. Webster also defines a cult as "a religion that is considered or held to be false or unorthodox. . ." Again we find that most anyone could charge anyone else with being a member of a cult if we use Webster's definition.

One of the world's foremost authorities relative to cults and Christianity, Dr. Walter Martin, defined a cult that I find acceptable in the context of the Christian religion. Dr. Martin says that cults are religious groups holding "to doctrines which are pointedly contradictory to orthodox Christianity and which yet claim the distinction of tracing their origin to orthodox sources." Obviously this definition is workable since the essential and operative construction of any religious belief must be its own doctrine. For instance, the definition of Christianity includes a wide variance of biblical doctrine. Christians have traditionally declared that certain doctrines are heretical. It is the heresy that leads to sectarianism. Once a sect is established, it is often called a cult. Dr. John Gerstner

18. Brief Comments

preferred to use 'sect' when referring to those Christian denominations not regarded as evangelical.... Those which do not hold to evangelical principles are not usually called churches at all, but sects or cults." It may be said that a cult rejects a major tenet of historical orthodox Christianity.

America has dug itself into the abyss of ignorance with the popular notion of freedom of speech and religion. A person can say anything about anyone and they often do, especially when it comes to religious matters. The average man is pitifully ignorant of theological propositions among the world religions. Unfortunately many people do not even understand the creeds and confessions of their own denominations. So how does one expect to understand the difference between the church, a sect, and a cult? It requires diligent study, meditation, and patience to sort out the orthodox from the heterodox. It is for that very reason that God has given "pastors and teachers, for the equipping of the saints for the work of ministry, for the edifying of the body of Christ, till we all come to the unity of the faith and of the knowledge of the Son of God. . ." (Ephesians 4:11ff). In Dr. Issac Watts' book entitled *The Improvement of the Mind* he reminds us "there are few persons of so penetrating a genius, and so just a judgment, as to be capable of learning the arts and sciences without the assistance of teachers. His assistance is absolutely necessary for most persons, and it is very useful for all beginners. Books are a sort of dumb teachers; they point out the way of learning; but if we labour under any doubt or mistake, they cannot answer sudden questions, or explain present doubts and difficulties: this is properly the work of a living instructor" (*The Improvement of the Mind*, by Issac Watts, pg. 62).

So the question is asked: What cults do we face in our nation? The answer is that there are too many to mention, so a couple of the major ones will suffice. We must remember that most of the cults are simply modern versions of ancient heresies faced by the early Christian church. The following are some examples taken from John Witmer's book, *Truth About Error*.

> The Christology of Christian Science, for example, is a modern expression of the docetic heresy the Apostle John refuted in his First Epistle (1:1-3 {1 John 1}; 4:1-3 {1 John 4}). The Christian Science emphasis upon the non-reality of evil, disease, and death comes from neo-Platonism, which rests in turn upon Platonic and Zoroastrian dualism with the concepts of the essential evilness of matter. The Christology of the Jehovah's Witnesses, on the other hand, is a modern form of Arianism proscribed as heretical by the Council of Nicea. Many of the contemporary heretical cults, furthermore, are imbued with the Judaistic and/or the Gnostic spirit that was confronted and refuted primarily by the Apostle Paul. The Sabbath-keeping, the dietary laws, and the legalism of Seventh-Day Adventism, for example, reflect the Judaistic spirit. On the other hand, the emphasis upon going beyond the simplicity of the Christian faith and becoming an initiate into special truths which is found among the Jehovah's Witnesses and also to some extent the Mormons reflect the spirit of Gnosticism (*Truth About Error,* by John Witmer).

Before calling any group a cult some serious study of their theology, doctrine, and practice should be considered and they should be challenged in a church council to defend their heresy.

About the Author

Martin Murphy has a B.A. in Bible from Columbia International University and Master of Divinity from Reformed Theological Seminary. Martin spent nearly thirty years in the class room, the pulpit, the lectern, the study, and the library. He now devotes most of his time consolidating academic and practical gains by writing books. He is the author of 18 other books.

More Books by Martin Murphy

The Church: First Thirty Years, 344 pages, ISBN 9780985618179, $15.95. This book is an exposition of the Book of Acts. It will help Christians understand the purpose, mission, and ministry of the church.

The Dominant Culture: Living in the Promised Land, 172 pages, ISBN 970991481118, $11.95. This book examines the culture of Israel during the period of the Judges. It explains how worldviews influence the church and it reveals biblical principles to help Christians learn how to live in the culture.

My Christian Apology, 98 pages, ISBN 9780984570874, $7.95. This book investigates the doctrine of Christian apologetics. It explains rational Christian apologetics.

The Essence of Christian Doctrine, 200 pages, ISBN 9780984570812, $12.95. This book was written so that pastors and layman would have a quick reference to major biblical doctrines. Dr. Steve Brown says it was written, "with clarity and power about the verities of the Christian faith and in a way that makes a difference in how we live."

Return to the Lord, 130 pages, ISBN 9780984570805, $8.95. This book is an exposition Hosea. The prophet speaks a message of repentance and hope. Hosea's prophetic message to Old Testament and New Testament congregation is "you have broken God's covenant; return to the Lord. Dr. Richard Pratt said "We need more correct and practical instruction in the prophetic books, and you have given us just that."

Theological Terms in Layman Language, 130 pages, ISBN 9780985618155, $8.95. This book is written so that simple words like faith or not so simple words like aseity are explained in plain language. Theological Terms in Layman Language is easy to read and designed for people who want a brief definition for theological terms. The terms are in layman friendly language.

Brief Study of the Ten Commandments, 164 pages, 9780991481163, $10.95. This book will help Christians discover or re-discover the meaning of the Ten Commandments.

Doctrine of Sound Words: Summary of Christian Theology, 424 pages, ISBN 9780991481125, $16.95. This explains the doctrine of Christianity in a systematic format for the layperson. It covers a wide range of theological topics such as, the triune God, creation, providence, sin, justification, repentance, Christian liberty, free will, marriage and divorce, Christian fellowship, et al). There are thirty three topics beginning with "Holy Scriptures" and ending with "The Last Judgment." It is a systematic theology for laymen based on the full counsel of God.

The god of the Church Growth Movement, 95 pages ISBN 9780986405587, $6.95. This work includes a brief explanation of modernity and its effect on church growth. It is a critical analysis of the church growth movement found in every branch of the Protestant church.

Friendship: The Joy of Relationships, 46 pages, ISBN 9780986405518, $6.49. This condensed book was written so the reader will be able to grasp the principles without having to go back and re-read it to digest the content. Friendship is a popular concept. Having a large number of friends was popularized by the social media such as Twitter and Facebook. Friendship involves a relationship of distinction. It is a relationship that respects the dignity of another person. The Bible teaches a different version of what it means to be a friend than the popular culture teaches.

Ultimate Authority for the Soul, 151 pages, ISBN 9780986405501, $9.99. This book examines that question and concludes that every rational being has some recognition of God as the ultimate authority. Although God is the ultimate authority, He confers His authority by means of the Word of God. The author examines Psalm 119 to build a defense for the ultimate authority for the soul.

Constitutional Authority in a Postmodern Culture, ISBN 9780985618124, 56 pages, $5.95. This book shows the validity of constitutional authority and the invasion of postmodern theories in western culture. Postmodern theory has assaulted the western culture on the battleground of absolute truth and reality. Postmodern theory places human experience over abstract objective principles. Christians have a constitution known as the Bible so they will know the truth of reality. The last chapter is devoted to cultural reformation.

Learn to Pray: Biblical Doctrine of Prayer, ISBN 9780986405563, 107 pages, $7.95. This book examines the Lord's model prayer so Christians may learn to pray according to the Lord's instruction. It also reviews some of the prayers of the apostle Paul to discover his doctrine of prayer. Pastor James Perry wrote the Foreword with insight and experience. "I am impressed with this book on the subject of Learn to Pray. It is stated briefly and succinctly following the model and example of the Lord's Prayer. There is considerable practical instruction on the meaning and implication about purposeful and biblical prayer and it will serve as a useful primer for all who apply the prayer principles. The reader will doubtlessly return to the instruction frequently for the practical help it offers."

God's Grace For the Church: Exposition of Ephesians, ISBN 9781732437906, 150 pages, $8.95. This exposition of Paul's letter to the church at Ephesus is readable, reasonable, and relevant. It brings the grace of God to the forefront of the Christian experience. The author simply lays out the plain teaching of Scripture. Martin does not avoid theological topics that are obviously in the text of Scripture, but he does not engage in contentious arguments. It is written for Christians who want to understand and experience the manifestation of God's grace. Pastor Clark Cornelius describes the book from a pastor's perspective. "With the storytelling of a historian, the compassion of a pastor, and the skill to make theology apply to daily living, Martin Murphy's Exposition of Ephesians guides the reader through a treasure house enumerating God's grace. It illuminates God's spiritual riches to a modern Church, which has forgotten Christ's wall-destroying work of unity. Murphy's work sounds the call for the modern Christian to embrace his pre-destiny, suit up for service, and enjoy God's gifts of grace and peace."

www.ingramcontent.com/pod-product-compliance
Lightning Source LLC
Chambersburg PA
CBHW071504040426
42444CB00008B/1483